DIGITAL LIBRARIES

DIGITAL LIBRARIES

Dr. P. Balasubramanian
M.A., M.B.A., M.C.A., M.L.I.Sc., M.Phil., PGDPR, Ph.D.
University Librarian
Manonmaniam Sundaranar University
Tirunelveli 627012
Tamil Nadu
India

Ess Ess Publications
New Delhi

Digital Libraries

ISBN : 978-93-87698-76-5

Price : Rs. 875/-

First Published 2020

Published by:
Ess Ess Publications
4831/24, Ansari Road,
Darya Ganj,
New Delhi-110 002.
INDIA
Phones: 23260807, 41563444
Fax: 41563334
E-mail: info@essessreference.com
www.essessreference.com

Cover Design by *Patch Creative Unit*

Printed and bound in India

Dedicated to
MY BELOVED PARENTS

Contents

Contents

Preface

The Basic Objective behind writing this book is to get knowledge from different tools of Libraries.

In this book I have included various concept, effects, process, types, overview and implication regarding library management. Subject matter of this topic has been elaborated with simple words.

I gave my complete effort to make it valuable, useful and enrich it with my views so that it give complete sense and benefit to readers. I hope who goes through it will find it interesting and worth reading. All constructive feedback is cordially invited.

Suggestion to new ideas for further improvement of this book shall be greatly appreciated and acknowledged.

— **Dr. P. Balasubramanian**

Acknowledgements

The author feels extremely indebted to Dr. K. Pitchumani, Honourable Vice-Chancellor, Manonmaniam Sundaranar University, Tirunelveli. We also thank Dr. S. Santhosh Baboo, Registrar, Manonmaniam Sundaranar University, Tirunelveli and all the teaching and non-teaching staff members of the M.S. University, for giving us constant encouragement in writing this book.

I acknowledge my heartfelt gratitude to Dr. P.Ravichandran, Professor & Head, Department of Library & Information Science, Annamalai University, Annamalai Nagar and Prof. Dr. A. Rangaswamy for his invaluable advice and suggestions.

I would also like to thank my friend Dr. R. Murugesan, Assistant Professor (T), Manonmaniam Sundaranar University, Tirunelveli for helping me in every possible manner in bringing out this book.

I acknowledge the services of Ess Ess Publications, New Delhi for their efforts in bringing out this book in a record time. Suggestions for further improvement of the book are most welcome.

— Dr. P. Balasubramanian

1
Concept of Digital Library

INTRODUCTION

A digital library is a highly organized collection of electronic resources. Digital libraries share an important characteristic with search engines - they can both be accessed online. However, while search engines cover a wide range of subject areas, digital libraries are more narrowly focused around one or a specific group of disciplines. Unlike search engines, digital libraries attach content-specific and highly descriptive metadata to describe each item in the collection. When a user conducts a search in the digital library it is this metadata that is searched. Search engines, on the other hand, search "blindly" on an item's content and the results obtained may only indicate that a particular search terms appears somewhere in the item, and not whether the overall content of the item is relevant to the search. Therefore, searches in a digital library produce more useful results, save users' time and effort in searching, and users can access the information found instantly. Digital library is a very complex and dynamic entity. It has brought phenomenal change in the information collection, preservation and dissemination scene of the world. There are many definitions and they are synonymously used as electronic library or virtual Library.

They require technology to link the resources of many and the linkage between them and the information services are transparent to the end users. Their collections are not limited to document surrogates they extend to digital artifacts that cannot be represented or distributed in printed formats. Another thing is that digital libraries will not be single, completely digital system that provides instant access to all information, for all sectors of society, from anywhere in the world. This is simply unrealistic. This concept comes from the early days when people were unaware of the complexities of building digital libraries. Instead, they will most likely be a collection of disparate resources and disparate systems, catering to specific communities and user groups, created for specific purposes. They also will include, perhaps indefinitely, paper-based collections.

Library and information centers are providing numerous types of information resources and services. Information content and services are changing with the passage of time. The global network internet has brought forth new dimension to libraries of modern digital world. In order to keep pace with the cyberspace librarians are to be furnished libraries with latest version of sophisticated technology. In this new library digital networking and communication infrastructure provides a global platform over which the people and organization devise strategies, interact, communicate, collaborate and search for information. This platform includes, a vast array of digitalizable products that is databases, news and information, books, magazines, TV and radio programming, movies, electronic games, musical CDs and software which are delivered over the digital infrastructure anytime, anywhere in the world.

Another factor adding to the confusion is that digital libraries are at the focal point of many different areas of research, and what constitutes a digital library differs depending upon the research community that is describing it (Nurnberg, et al, 1995). For example:

- From an information retrieval point of view, it is a large database
- For people who work on hypertext technology, it is one particular application of hypertext methods
- For those working in wide-area information delivery, it is an application of the Web
- And for library science, it is another step in the continuing automation of libraries that began over 25 years ago

In fact, a digital library is all of these things. These different research approaches will all add to the development of digital libraries.

Third, confusion arises from the fact that there are many things on the Internet that people are calling "digital libraries," which from a librarian's point of view are not. For example:

- For computer scientists and software developers, collections of computer algorithms or software programs are digital libraries.
- For database vendors or commercial document suppliers, their databases and electronic document delivery services and digital libraries.
- For large corporations, a digital library is the document management systems that control their business documents in electronic form.
- For a publisher, it may be an online version of a catalogue.
- And for at least one very large software company, a digital library is the collection of whatever it can

buy the rights to, and then charge people for using.

Objectives

- To facilitate the development of strategies and guidelines for the preservation of access to digital information;
- To define and conduct a joint program of activities in order to integrate and coordinate the on-going research activities of the major research teams in the field of digital libraries for the purpose of developing the next generation digital library technologies;
- To contribute improving the effectiveness of research in the digital library field;

HISTORY OF DEVELOPMENT OF DIGITAL LIBRARIES

The historical significance of digital publishing is equivalent to that of printed material and has significant effects on every aspect of the future of library and information professionals. Digital libraries have transformed the basic function of the library that of meeting the information needs of the user. Paradigm change is being witnessed in the ways information is being produced, delivered and accessed.

The origin of the digital library can be traced back to the writings of H G Wells (1938), the well-known English science fiction pioneer specially in 'World Brain' (Wells, 1938) a collection of essays where he introduced the concept of World Encyclopedia. The concept of Memex in 'As We May Think', an essay byVannevar Bush, first published in The Atlantic Monthly, m July 1945(Bush, 1945). Engelbart (1962), an early computer and Internet pioneer best known for his work on the challenges of humancomputer interaction, reasoned that the state of our current technology controls our ability to manipulate information, and that fact in turn will control our ability to develop new, improved technologies. Thus, he set himself to the revolutionary task of developing computer-based technologies for processing information directly and also to improve individual and group processes for knowledge work.

Engelbart's philosophy and research agenda is most clearly and directly expressed in his research report. Licklider (1965) in his book 'Libraries of the future' (1965) puts his networked systems theories together for information service and retrieval and argued that libraries may be replaced by computers in the future. The contribution of the above stalwarts has a lot of impact on the present day digital libraries. Providing access to information sources in response to user requests has seen the libraries transitioning from collecting material to developing policies for doing the same. This has resulted in the new phenomenon of 'just in time' from the age old 'just in case' to cater to the user's needs.

The shift to on-demand delivery can be facilitated by providing access to digital material from any source and any place. This digital transition has resulted in research being undertaken on various aspects of building digital library. So all sources where the information is available in electronic formats and accessible with the help of computers is referred in a wider perspective as 'electronic information resources' and encompass terms like automated library, electronic library, virtual library, networked library, multimedia library.

All these are being used interchangeably and synonymously. But the term 'digital library' has become the preferred term due to the integration of mission, techniques and cultures of physical libraries with the abilities and culture of computing and tele-communications. Since digital information can be delivered directly to the user, and can be used simultaneously by many, is cost effective, has sophisticated searching and fast retrieval is well established and understood. The last two decades has witnessed the spurt of Digital Library Initiatives all over the world. Most of them are a result of the digital library research and development activities.

CONCEPTS OF DIGITAL LIBRARY

As defined by Reitz (2008), digitization is "the process of converting data to digital format for processing by a computer. In information systems, digitization usually refers to the conversion of printed text or images (photographs, illustrations, maps, etc.) into binary signals using some kind of scanning device that enables the result to be displayed on a computer screen." She also defines digital library as the "library in which a significant proportion of the resources are available in machine-readable format (as opposed to print or micro-form), accessible by means of computers".

The digital libraries store, organize and disseminate digital contents. These contents are created either through digitization of existing printed materials and media documents, or through re-keying/re-composing of existing printed materials and media documents, or through creating new documents in digital formats. The first kind of documents is known as digitized documents, and the later kind of documents is known as born digital documents. In Indian digital libraries both kinds of documents are available. The digitized documents are stored either in image formats or in text formats. If the original documents are available in European languages such as English, French, German and Spanish, the optical character recognition (OCR) software can automatically convert them into searchable digital text format, where qualitative OCR conversion rate is much higher. On the other hand, if the original documents are available in Indian languages such as Sanskrit, Hindi, Bengali, Oriya, Telugu and Tamil, the contents are made available either in image formats or re-keying the texts for the inclusion in the digital libraries. OCR software for Indian languages is still in the developmental or testing stage, where OCR conversion rate is much lower than acceptable rate. The full-text searching is possible in textual documents but this facility is absent in image documents.

DOCUMENTS AND COLLECTIONS IN DIGITAL LIBRARY SYSTEMS.

Digital library is the concept of information stored digitally and made accessible to users through digital systems and networks, but having no single location. It is, therefore, analogous to a library as a storehouse of information, but has a virtual existence in the digital spaces. Digital library is essentially a fully automated information system with all resources in digital form. Many views of digital libraries stem from what libraries currently do. Traditional libraries collect, organize, provide access to, and preserve objects in their collections. A library collection may include books, magazines, journals, theses, dissertations, manuscripts, audio-visuals, maps, etc. The flexibility of digital technology allows it to handle new kinds of object efficiently. Digital library collections can include things without direct physical analogs, such as algorithms or real time data feeds. They also may include digitized representations of what have traditionally appeared largely in museums and archives. With the rise of cost of paper publications and library storage, increasing use of computers, decreasing budgets, many libraries have to reduce their acquisition of books as well as their journal subscriptions. Documents in electronic form can become more easily available and widely used because the cost of digital storage and processing is going down.

Documents are the heart of digital libraries. Without documents there would be no digital libraries. In digital libraries, documents are not only what are stored in traditional libraries (e.g., books, journals, pictures and videos), but also include many works uncommon to those libraries, e.g., multilingual, multimedia, and structured documents (e.g., books broken into chapters, sections, subsections, figures with attached captions, colour graphics or images, attached or linked sound or video files, appendices, indexes, and 'front matter'); programs, algorithms, bulletin board archives, besides others. A document can have various representations depending on its intended use; for example, some applications require high-resolution images of documents with invisible watermarks for security purposes as well as low-resolution images for children to download from the Internet. Collections of digital library ranges from small, self-contained, and narrowly defined collections to ones spread across physical and logical spaces. One of the common requirements for a digital library is the ability to deal with distributed collections of information.

EVALUATION OF DIGITIZATION WORK AND DIGITAL LIBRARY SYSTEM

A digital library may be evaluated from a number of perspectives, such as collaboration pattern, system, access and usability, user interfaces, information retrieval, content and domain, services, cost and overall benefits and impact. An important issue under discussion across various communities is the set of metrics to be used for evaluating digital libraries. Selection of digital library metrics should be considered from both system-oriented and user-oriented viewpoints. From the system's perspective, we consider capacity (number of digital objects stored and number of users served simultaneously), content, transaction speed (speed of search response). From the user's perspective, we consider impacts of the system on the user (e.g., impact on patterns of association and attitudes about the digital libraries), effectiveness (relevance of the results; ability to produce a ranked list of results that are mostly relevant with best matches at the top), usability (e.g., ease of use, suitability to purpose, user's effort), interactions with the system, and user satisfaction.

In a general way, the constructs or elements for evaluation of digitization projects covered in this study are:

- Collaboration pattern for collection building;
- Collaboration pattern for resources mobilization and utilization;
- Selection of contents for digitization;
- Digitization workflow;
- Interpretation, representation and metadata;
- Access and distribution — open access versus campus-wide (closed) access;
- User interfaces — search and retrieval; and
- Integration, cooperation with other resources and libraries.

FIVE LAWS OF LIBRARY SCIENCE WITH DIGITAL LIBRARY

A digital library is the infrastructure, policies and procedures, and organizational, political and economic mechanisms necessary to enable access to and preservation of digital content. In some instances a digital library may be a new entity, but in most cases it will be the electronic or digital face of a traditional library and its activities will be embedded within current and evolving service structures.

Ranganathan (1999) uses his five laws to drive the classification and management of printed information. He started the classic five laws of library science as a sprit behind architecting and managing the libraries. We shall attempt to arrive at frameworks and structures that will help as build future digital information systems. The same five laws of library science may be rephrased as given below with somewhat different relative emphasis to guide us in architecting managing digital information systems of the 21st century:

1. Digital resources are for use.
2. Every user seeks digital resource.
3. Every digital resource needs its user.
4. Save the time of the user.
5. Digital library is a growing organism worldwide.

TRANSITION OF LIBRARIES FROM TRADITIONAL TO DIGITAL

The tools used by librarians in their daily work have changed vastly during recent years. Today, hardly any library is equipped exactly as it was only a few years ago. In addition to traditional means like card catalogues and microfiche readers, most libraries now also offer an online public access catalogue (OPAC), public PCs equipped with CD-ROM drives, scanners, or public terminals connected to the Internet. An increasing number of libraries are building homepages on the World Wide Web from where users have access to a variety of services without physically entering a library.

Many libraries are in transit from the traditional towards the digital library. We witness a shift from libraries offering information about (electronic and print) information towards providing access to full texts of documents. Not only recent publications, but also many historical library holdings are being digitized (see e.g., Corbin and Coletti, 1995). These electronic collections allow users from everywhere at any time to consult the material without doing any harm to fragile documents.

Despite numerous digitization projects, electronic media by no means are dominant compared to print material. There is still a lot of paper in our libraries, and we expect this to be the case for a long time to come. The paper-based library will co-exist with the digital library for the foreseeable future, because electronic publications are not developing at the expense of print media, but in addition to them.

The notion of library has long expanded beyond the physical building of the library. Our services always included access to sources that are physically located outside the library. Over the course of the years, librarians have collaborated in many ways. Central cataloguing, union lists of journals, cooperative collection development and interlibrary loan are only a few examples of resource sharing. Forced by decreasing budgets, many libraries have redefined their acquisitions policy from purchasing documents "just in case" to "just in time", since no library can afford to purchase every item that might be needed by one user one day. Through collaboration and reciprocal services among libraries, we can provide a much larger range of resources to our users and fulfil their information needs quicker, cheaper, and more completely than one library alone would be able to do.

While projects that aim at helping each other might be seen as a nicety during prosperous years and become a necessity in times of economic restraints, they play an ever more essential role in the electronic environment. James Michael suggested a blueprint for the library without walls that consisted of five elements (Michael, 1994):

- interconnectivity - connecting to a network
- interoperability - the ability of one computer to talk to another
- integration - of internal and external resources into one single user interface
- intermediation - reference services, navigational help and instruction provided by librarians
- interdependency - because one single library cannot own all the resources that might ever be needed by users

This last item, interdependency, is the final step for the "Global Digital Library" to become reality. In the electronic environment, even more than in the traditional paper-based world, no library can (or may) store all the documents to which it provides access. Digital libraries are only possible if reliable partners cooperate on a long-term basis. Authors, libraries, publishers, archives - the concept of one player in the electronic publishing sector as a self-sufficient entity has been overcome for good. The digital library indeed brings us closer together than ever.

Digital libraries – definition

The Digital Library definitions are numerous. The spectrum of possible meanings for the term is "ranging from a digitized collection of material that one might find in a traditional library through to the collection of all digital information along with the services that make that information useful to all possible users".

Here are some definitions:

"Digital libraries are organized collections of digital information. They combine the structuring and gathering of information, which libraries and archives have always done, with the digital representation that computers have made possible".

"A digital library is a collection of information that is stored and accessed electronically".

"A digital library is the technologies, tools, resources, and practices associated with the management of content in an electronic information environment".

"An informal definition of a digital library is a managed collection of information, with associated services, where the information is stored in digital formats and accessible over a network. A crucial part of this definition is that the information is managed. A stream of data sent to earth from a satellite is not a library. The same data, when organized systematically, becomes a digital library collection".

"The digital library is not merely equivalent to a

digitized collection with information management tools. It is also a series of activities that brings together collections, services, and people in support of the full life cycle of creation, dissemination, use, and preservation of data, information, and knowledge".

A digital library is "a managed environment of multimedia materials in digital form, designed for the benefit of its user population, structured to facilitate access to its contents and equipped with aids to navigation of the global network".

"A digital library contains digital representations of the objects found in it - most understanding of the digital library probably also assumes that it will be accessible via the Internet, though not necessarily to everyone. But the idea of digitization is perhaps the only characteristic of a digital library on which there is universal agreement".

"A digital library is an electronic extension of functions users typically perform and the resources they access in a traditional library".

"A digital library encompasses two possibilities: a) library that contains material in digitized form, and b) library that contains digital material. There is a subtle difference between the two (though not of great significance). In first case, the digital content is produced by digitizing physical counterparts (e.g. paper). In the second case, the initial content itself is created in digital form".

"A digital library is the collection of services and the collection of information objects that support users in dealing with information objects and the organization and presentation of those objects available directly or indirectly via electronic/digital means".

The elements that have been identified as common to the many definitions are that the digital library is a collection of digital information that has to be manageable, that it includes services and activities needed for its functionality and that a universal access to digital libraries and information services is a goal. The most authors agree that a digital library must comprise three central aspects: first - an availability of digital data in a large extent, second – regional independence, third – an improved access to the data through a common interface and added value services for the user. A fully developed digital library environment usually involves the functions of the initial conversion of content from physical to digital form. Other important elements are the extraction or creation of metadata or indexing information describing the content to enable the function of searching, and administrative and structural metadata to help to maintain other services, such as viewing, management, and preservation. Further, there must be an appropriate multimedia repository available for the storage of digital content and metadata. Other important elements are client services for the browser, including repository querying and workflow, content delivery via file transfer or streaming media and a private or public network.

Along with the term "digital library", there are relative terms "electronic library" and "virtual library". The term "electronic library" appeared in the mid -70s, the term "virtual library" emerged later – somewhat around 1980, and the term "digital library" is the youngest and at the time the most popular one. The notion "digital library" gained its importance in the tight coherence with the World Wide Web. In most cases, the 3 terms are applied fully synonym to each other. As to the differences between these notions: electronic library is in some cases seen as a part of the digital library in the way that an electronic library is a collection of materials in a digital form. A virtual library can also be seen as a part of a digital library, as it is a library that is independent of any locations. Sometimes an electronic library is seen as a preliminary stage of a virtual library. A virtual library is mostly comprehended as a library without walls. An electronic library can consist of both electronic and conventional part, or just be a library with computer assistance. Another term "hybrid library" is mostly used to stress the fact that the library consists of both conventional and virtual/digital parts. A restriction of the term "digital library" from the other types is very difficult. To avoid complicity, we shall only work with the term "digital library", under which we shall understand a large collection of digital materials, which is regionally independent, and which offers a number of integrated digital services under a uniform user interface, and drop its synonyms.

Characteristics

Cleveland (1998) describes some characteristics of digital libraries that have been gleaned from various discussions about digital libraries (Digital Libraries), both online and in print:

- Digital Libraries are the digital face of traditional libraries that include both digital collections and traditional, fixed media collections. So they encompass both electronic and paper materials.
- Digital Libraries will also include digital materials that exist outside the physical and administrative bounds of any one digital library
- Digital Libraries will include all the processes and services that are the backbone and nervous system of libraries. However, such traditional processes, though forming the basis digital library work, will have to be revised and enhanced to accommodate the differences between new digital media and traditional fixed media.
- Digital Libraries ideally provide a coherent view of all of the information contained within a library, no matter its form or format
- Digital Libraries will serve particular communities or constituencies, as traditional libraries do now,

though those communities may be widely dispersed throughout the network.

- Digital Libraries will require both the skills of librarians and well as those of computer scientists to be viable.

Cleveland (1998) believes that this definition of a digital library, and these characteristics, are the most logical because it expands and extends the traditional library, preserves the valuable work that they do, while integrating new technologies, new processes, and new media.

PRINCIPLES OF DIGITAL LIBRARY

Building a digital library is expensive and resource-intensive. Before embarking on such a venture, it is important to consider some basic principles underlying the design, implementation, and maintenance of any digital library. These principles apply not only to conversion projects in which analogy objects are converted to digital form, but to digital libraries in which the objects have always been in digital form ("born digitally") and to "mixed" digital libraries in which the objects may be of both types. The principles are, in some sense, self-evident, yet it is easy to lose sight of them when under pressure to build a system, despite limited resources and time. The purpose of a digital library is to provide coherent organization and convenient access to typically large amounts of digital information. The following 10 principles are helps to design and continued development of any digital library system. They are:

1. Expect change.
2. Know your content.
3. Involve the right Jie Sun and Bao-Zhong Yuan / IERI Procedia 2 (2012) 12 – 17 15 people.
4. Design usable systems.
5. Ensure open access.

6. Be aware of data rights.
7. Automate whenever possible.
8. Adopt and adhere to standards.
9. Ensure quality.
10. Be concerned about persistence.

Functions of Digital Library

The rapid development of the internet in the 1990s and its embrace by the library and information community enabled the concept of the digital libraries (DLs), whose function can be defined as the collection, storage and processing of vast information and knowledge into a systemic project through digitalization and the internet, while providing convenient and highly efficient retrieval and inquiry services. To this effect, at a minimum, the core services expected of a Digital Library System include: a repository service for storing and managing digital objects; a search service to facilitate information discovery; and a user interface through which end users interact with the digital objects. The introduction of the DL has raised library modernization to a new level with over time. Digital libraries promise new societal benefits, starting with the elimination of the time and space constraints of traditional bricks-and-mortar libraries. Unlike libraries that occupy buildings accessible only to those who walk through their doors, digital libraries reside on inter-networked data storage and computing systems that can be accessed by people located anywhere. At their full potential digital libraries will enable any citizen to access a considerable proportion of all human knowledge from any location. From an access vantage the Internet provides a preview of the possibilities. The role of a Digital Library is essentially to collect, manage, preserve and make accessible digital objects. The following are some of the function of digital library:

1. To provide friendly interface to users.

2. To avail network facilities.
3. To support library functions.
4. To enhance advanced search, access and retrieval of information.
5. To improve the library operations.
6. To enable one to perform searches that is not practical manually.
7. To protect owners of information.
8. To preserve unique collection through digitization.

BENEFITS OF DIGITAL LIBRARIES

Digitalization can offer many advantages to libraries as well as to their users. The benefits mentioned by T.B. Rajashekar are the following:

- Digital libraries make it needless for the user to go somewhere. A user can get full information at home or at work, whenever there is a PC and a network collection.
- Information can be updated continuously much more easily. It easier to keep the information current.
- An important benefit offered by digital libraries is searching and browsing in material. One can optimize searching and simultaneously search the Internet, commercial databases, and library collections. Then one can save search results and conduct additional processing to narrow or qualify results, or click through search results to access the digitized content or locate additional items of interest.
- Information can be shared with others more easily. By placing digital information on a server connected to the World Wide Web makes it available to everyone.
- Duplicating of information is easy and cheap, whereas duplication of paper material would be very expensive.

- Digital libraries compared to conventional libraries allow collaboration and exchange of ideas.
- Arising new forms of information: information in digital form can support features and possibilities not given in print form.
- Digital libraries are cost-saving, since expensive building, professional staff and maintenance demanded by conventional libraries not needed anymore.

THEORETICAL FUNDAMENTALS

The 5S Framework is the result of an activity aimed at defining digital libraries in a rigorous manner. It is based on five fundamental abstractions, namely Streams, Structures, Spaces, Scenarios and Societies. These five concepts are informally defined as follows:

- Streams are sequences of elements of an arbitrary type (e.g. bits, characters, images) and thus they can model both static and dynamic content. Static streams correspond to information content represented as basic elements, e.g. a simple text is a sequence of characters, while a complex object like a book may be a stream of simple text and images. Dynamic streams are used to model any information flow and thus are important for representing any communication that takes place in the digital library. Finally, streams are typed and the type is used to define their semantics and application area.
- Structures are the way through which parts of a whole are organized. In particular, they can be used to represent hypertexts and structured information objects, taxonomies, system connections and user relationships.
- Spaces are sets of objects together with operations on those objects conforming to certain constraints.

This type of construct is powerful and, as suggested by the conceivers, when a part of a DL cannot be well described using another of the 5S concepts, space may well be applicable. Document spaces are the key concepts in digital libraries. However, spaces are used in various contexts – e.g. indexing and visualizing – and different types of spaces are proposed, e.g. measurable spaces, measure spaces, probability spaces, vector spaces and topological spaces.

- Scenarios are sequences of events that may have parameters, and events represent state transitions. The state is determined by the content in a specific location but the value and the location are not investigated further because these aspects are system dependent. Thus a scenario tells what happens to the streams in spaces and through the structures. When considered together, the scenarios describe the services, the activities and the tasks representing digital library functions. DL workflows and data flows are examples of scenarios.
- Societies are sets of entities and relationships. The entities may be humans or software and hardware components, which either use or support digital library services. Thus, society represents the highest-level concept of a Digital Library, which exists to serve the information needs of its societies and to describe the context of its use.

TASKS AND SERVICES OF DIGITAL LIBRARIES

Digital libraries provide and extend traditional library services in the digital environment. A digital library can offer a number of additional value added services, which are not offered by conventional libraries. Here are some examples, provided by Endres and Fellner:

1. A time-restricted access to a certain document can be provided instead of delivering a title; sometimes

exactly this form of document access might be needed. Personalization through profile service can be offered. This service gives the user a possibility to hand over the profile of his interests in form of a list of key words. The library then uses this profile to pick out those documents out of the new comings, which may be interesting for the user. This service is also often called the Selective Dissemination of Information.

2. A digital library might enable a notification service. A user can be notified per some means of communication whenever a new title – article or a book - appears in a catalog, or a new registry in a database, which matches the interests of the user.
3. Creation of thesaurus and classification schemes are next important instruments for description and searching for information offered by digital libraries.
4. Personal work space is a useful feature. It is adjusted for the needs of a particular user. An example could be a working space, which allows the user to use text processing, mathematical, statistical or graphical programs of a certain type.

DIGITAL LIBRARIES CREATIONS

One of the largest issues in creating digital libraries will be the building of digital collections. Digital imaging is an inter-linked system of hardware, software, image database, and access sub-system with each having their own components. Tools used for the digital library include several core and peripherals systems like hardware (such as scanners, computers, and data storage), software (image capturing and editing), network (data transmission), and display/printing technologies. Some of the important points to be considered in developing a digital library are as follows:

a. Digital collection : There are essentially three

methods of building digital collections:

(i) Digitization, converting paper and other media in existing collections to digital form

(ii) Acquisition of original digital works created by publishers and scholars. Example items would be electronic books, journals, and datasets.

(iii) Access to external materials not held in-house by providing pointers to websites, other library collections, or publishers' servers.

b. Access to external digital collection : The digital libraries can obtain access permission to digital collection provided by external sources like institutions, resources of the libraries, electronic journal through on-line access like Elsevier, ACM, etc., which provides their journals on-line through websites.

c. Access to digital information available on the web : WWW is the repositories of information and one of the important services of the internet. www.edoc.com, mel.library.mi.us, www.inflibnet.ac.in, etc., are the important portal sites or gateways that provide access to electronics resources. In this respect, we can say that digital libraries can provide access to electronic resources through library home page.

d. Conversion of print to digital : Mainly scanning and use of OCR programs and re-keying of data are the two important methods for converting the print to digital resources. Some of the technical requirements of the digital image processing include hardware (computer, scanner, input/output devices), software (image capturing, data compression/decompression), network (for transferring information for resource sharing), and display technologies. All the above components are the important machines and tools needed for digitization.

ADVANTAGES OF THE DIGITAL LIBRARY

Traditional libraries are limited by storage space;

digital libraries have the potential to store much more information, simply because digital information requires very little physical space to contain it. As such, the cost of maintaining a digital library is much lower than that of a traditional library. A traditional library must spend large sums of money paying for staff, book maintenance, rent, and additional books. Digital libraries do away with these fees. Digital library has certain characteristics, which make them different from traditional library. It has expansive and accurate system of searching with large volumes of text, image and audio-video resources. Digital libraries do not need physical space to build collection and it can be accessed from anywhere, any time. The user can get his/ her information on his own computer screen by using the Internet. Actually it is a network of multimedia system, which provides fingertip access. The following are some of the major advantages of digital libraries.

No physical boundary. The user of a digital library need not to go to the library physically; people from all over the world can gain access to the same information, as long as an Internet connection is available.

1. Round the clock availability. People can gain access to the information at any time, night or day.
2. Multiple accesses. The same resources can be used at the same time by a number of users. Structured approach. Digital libraries provide access to much richer content in a more structured manner, i.e. we can easily move from the catalog to the particular book then to a particular chapter and so on.
3. Information retrieval. The user is able to use any search term (word, phrase, title, name, subject) to search the entire collection. Digital libraries can provide very user friendly interfaces, giving clickable access to its resources.
4. Preservation and conservation. Another important issue is preservation - keeping digital information

available in perpetuity. In the preservation of digital materials, the real issue is technical obsolescence. Technical obsolescence in the digital age is like the deterioration of paper in the paper age. Libraries in the pre-digital era had to worry about climate control and the de-acidification of books, but the preservation of digital information will mean constantly coming up with new technical solutions.

5. Space. Whereas traditional libraries are limited by storage space, digital libraries have the potential to store much more information, simply because digital information requires very little physical space to contain them. When a library has no space for extension digitization is the only solution.
6. Networking. A particular digital library can provide a link to any other resources of other digital libraries very easily; thus a seamlessly integrated resource sharing can be achieved.
7. Cost. In theory, the cost of maintaining a digital library is lower than that of a traditional library. A traditional library must spend large sums of money paying for staff, book maintenance, rent, and additional books. Although digital libraries do away with these fees, it has since been found that digital libraries can be no less expensive in their own way to operate. Digital libraries can and do incur large costs for the conversion of print materials into digital format, for the technical skills of staff to maintain them, and for the costs of maintaining online access (i.e. servers, bandwidth costs, etc.). Also, the information in a digital library must often be "migrated" every few years to the latest digital media. This process can incur very large costs in hardware and skilled personnel.

And Chore and Salwe (2010) also give the advantages of digital library as:

1. Preserve the valuable documents, rare and special collections of libraries, archives and museums.
2. Protected information source.
3. Facility for the downloading and printing.
4. Provide faster access to the holding of libraries worldwide through automated better catalogues.
5. Help to locate both physical and digitized versions of scholarly articles and books through single interface.
6. Search optimization, simultaneous searches of the Internet make possible, preparing commercial databases and library collections.
7. The user can peruse them instant.
8. Cross references to other documents.
9. Making short the chain from author to user.
10. Save preparation/conservation cost, space and money.
11. Digital technology affords multiple, simultaneous user from a single original which are not possible for materials stored in any other forms.
12. Full text search.

DISADVANTAGES OF THE DIGITAL LIBRARY

The computer viruses, lack of standardization for digitized information, quick degrading properties of digitized material, different display standard of digital product and its associated problem, health hazard nature of the radiation from monitor etc. makes digital libraries at times handicap.

1. Copyright : Digitization violates the copy right law as the thought content of one author can be freely transfer by other without his acknowledgement. So one difficulty to overcome for digital libraries is the way to distribute information. How does a digital library distribute information at will while protecting the copyright of the author?

2. Speed of access : As more and more computer are connected to the Internet its speed of access reasonably decreasing. If new technology will not evolve to solve the problem then in near future Internet will be full of error messages.

3. Initial cost is high : The infrastructure cost of digital library i.e. the cost of hardware, software; leasing communication circuit is generally very high.

4. Band width : Digital library will need high band for transfer of multimedia resources but the band width is decreasing day by day due to its over utilization.

5. Efficiency : With the much larger volume of digital information, finding the right material for a specific task becomes increasingly difficult.

6. Environment : Digital libraries cannot reproduce the environment of a traditional library. Many people also find reading printed material to be easier than reading material on a computer screen.

7. Preservation : Due to technological developments, a digital library can rapidly become out-of-date and its data may become inaccessible.

CHALLENGES OF THE DIGITAL LIBRARY

The optimism and hype from the early 1990's has been replaced by a realization that building digital libraries will be a difficult, expensive, and long-term effort (Lynch and Garcia-Molina, 1995). Creating effective digital libraries poses serious challenges. The integration of digital media into traditional collections will not be straight-forward, like previous new media (e.g., video and audio tapes), because of the unique nature of digital information¾ it is less fixed, easily copied, and remotely accessible by multiple users simultaneously. Some the more serious issues facing the development of digital libraries are outlined below.

1. Technical architecture : The first issue is that of the technical architecture that underlies any digital library system. Libraries will need to enhance and upgrade current technical architectures to accommodate digital materials. The architecture will include components such as:

- high-speed local networks and fast connections to the Internet
- relational databases that support a variety of digital formats
- full text search engines to index and provide access to resources
- a variety of servers, such as Web servers and FTP servers
- Electronic document management functions that will aid in the overall management of digital resources.

One important thing to point out about technical architectures for digital libraries is that they won't be monolithic systems like the turn-key, single box OPAC's with which librarians are most familiar. Instead, they will be a collection of disparate systems and resources connected through a network, and integrated within one interface, most likely a Web interface or one of its descendants. For example, the resources supported by the architecture could include:

- bibliographic databases that point to both paper and digital materials
- indexes and finding tools
- collections of pointers to Internet resources
- directories
- primary materials in various digital formats
- photographs
- numerical data sets
- and electronic journals

Though these resources may reside on different systems and in different databases, they would appear as though there were one single system to the users of a particular community. Within a coordinated digital library scheme, some common standards will be needed to allow digital libraries to interoperate and share resources. The problem, however, is that across multiple digital libraries, there is a wide diversity of different data structures, search engines, interfaces, controlled vocabularies, document formats, and so on. Because of this diversity, federating all digital libraries nationally or internationally would an impossible effort. Thus, the first task would be to find sound reasons for federating particular digital libraries into one system. Narrowing the field in such a manner would reduce the technical and political hurdles required to establish common practices. Further, because of the often uncertain futures of both de jure and defacto standards over time, what those standards are is unclear.

2. Building digital collections : One of the largest issues in creating digital libraries will be the building of digital collections. Obviously, for any digital library to be viable, it must eventually have a digital collection with the critical mass to make it truly useful. There are essentially three methods of building digital collections:

1. Digitization, converting paper and other media in existing collections to digital form (discussed in more detail below).
2. Acquisition of original digital works created by publishers and scholars. Example items would be electronic books, journals, and datasets.
3. Access to external materials not held in-house by providing pointers to Web sites, other library collections, or publishers' servers.

While the third method may not exactly constitute part of a local collection, it is still a method of increasing the materials available to local users. One of main issues here is the degree to which libraries will digitize existing materials and acquire original digital works, as opposed to simply pointing to them externally. This a reprise of the old access versus ownership issue- but in the digital realm- with many of the same concerns such as:

- local control of collections
- long-term access and preservation

What about digital collection building in a coordinated scheme? There are many reasons why building digital collections is a good candidate for coordinated activity. First, acquiring digital works and doing in-house digitization are expensive, especially to undertake alone. By working together, institutions with common goals can gain greater efficiencies and reduce the overall costs involved in these activities, as was the case with retrospective conversion of bibliographic records. Second, it also reduces the redundancy and waste of acquiring or converting materials more than once. Third, coordinated digital collection building enhances resource sharing and increases the richness of collections to which users have access. How can specific materials to be processed by a given institution be identified? Who collects and/or digitizes what materials could be based on factors such as:

Collection strengths : A particular library with a strong collection focus could be responsible for digitizing selected portions of it and adding new digital works to it.

Unique collections : If a library has the only copies of something, they are obviously the ones to digitize it

The priorities of user communities : Such priorities will justify holding the materials locally, for example, because of the demands of a curriculum.

Manageable portions of collections : When there are no other overriding criteria, then material can be divided up among institutions simply according to what is reasonable for any one institution to collect or digitize.

Technical architecture : The state of a library's technical architecture will also be factor in selecting who digitizes what. A library must have a technical architecture up to the task of support a particular digital collection.

Skills of staff : Institutions whose staffs don't have the necessary skills can't become a major node in a national scheme.

Yet, no matter how a collection is built of materials digitized in-house, of original digital works, or of providing access to materials by pointing to other external resources libraries in a collective must ensure it is preserved and made available in perpetuity. For example, if the only copies of digital works reside on a particular publisher's server, then what happens if the publisher goes bankrupt? Or if the market value of a particular work approaches zero? What if all of part of a digital collection of a library was lost, such as through some catastrophic event? Ensuring long-term preservation and access will require policies and a scheme by which redundant permanent copies are stored at designated institutions. Preservation issues will be discussed further later in the paper.

3. Digitization : Recall that one of the primary methods of digital collection building is digitization. What does this term mean exactly? Simply put, it is the conversion of any fixed or analogue media such as books, journal articles, photos, paintings, microforms into electronic form through scanning, sampling, or in fact even re-keying. An obvious obstacle to digitization is that it is very expensive. One estimate from the University of Michigan at Ann Arbor, the organization responsible for the JSTOR project, puts the cost of digitizing a single page at $2 to $6 dollars US (Chepesuik, 1997:48).

How do you go about deciding what parts of a collection to digitize? There are several approaches available, at least theoretically:

Retrospective conversion of collections : essentially, starting at A and ending up a Z. However ideal such complete conversion would be, it is impractical or impossible technically, legally, and economically. This approach can arguably be dispensed with as a pipe dream.

Digitization of a particular special collection or a portion of one : A small collection of manageable size, and which is highly valued, is a prime candidate.

Highlight a diverse collection : by digitizing particularly good examples of some collection strength.

High-use materials : making those materials that are in most demand more accessible.

An ad hoc approach : where one digitizes and stores materials as they are requested. This is, however, a haphazard method of digital collection building.

These approaches can be used alone or in combination depending upon a particular institution's goals for digitization.

Nested within these approaches are several criteria for selecting individual items. These include:

- their potential for long-term use
- their intellectual or cultural value
- whether they provide greater access than possible with original materials (e.g., fragile, rare materials)
- and whether copyright restrictions or licensing will permit conversion.

4. Metadata : Metadata is another issue central to the development of digital libraries. Metadata is the data the describes the content and attributes of any particular item in a digital library. It is a concept familiar to librarians because it is one of the primary things that librarians do they create cataloguing records that describe documents. Metadata is important in digital libraries because it is the key to resource discovery and use of any document. Anyone who has used Alta Vista, Excite, or any of the other search engines on the Internet knows that simple full-text searches don't scale in a large network. One can get thousands of hits, but most of them will be irrelevant. While there are formal library standards for metadata, namely AACR, such records are very time-consuming to create and require specially trained personnel. Human cataloguing, though superior, is just too laboured extensive for the already large and rapidly expanding information environment. Thus, simpler schemes for metadata are being proposed as solutions.

While they are still in their infancy, a number of schemes have emerged, the most prominent of which is the Dublin Core, an effort to try and determine the "core" elements needed to describe materials. The first workshop took place at OCLC headquarters in Dublin, Ohio, hence the name "Dublin Core." The Dublin Core workshops defined a set of fifteen metadata elements much simpler than those used in traditional library cataloguing. They were designed to be simple enough to be used authors, but at the same time, descriptive enough to be useful in resource discovery.

The lack of common metadata standards ideally, defined for use in some specified context is yet another barrier to information access and use in a digital library, or in a coordinated digital library scheme.

5. Naming, identifiers, and persistence : The fifth issue is related to metadata. It is the problem of naming in a digital library. Names are strings that uniquely identify digital objects and are part of any document's metadata. Names are as important in a digital library as an ISBN number is in a traditional library. They are needed to uniquely identify digital objects for purposes such as:

- citations
- information retrieval
- to make links among objects
- and for the purposes of managing copyright

Any system of naming that is developed must be permanent, lasting indefinitely. This means, among other things, that the name can't be bound up with a specific location. The unique name and its location must be separate. This is very much unlike URLs, the current method for identifying objects on the Internet. URL's confound in one string several items that should be separate. They include the method by which a document is accessed (e.g., HTTP), a machine name and document path (its location), and a document file name which may or may not be unique (e.g., how many index.html files do you have on your Web site?). URLs are very bad names because whenever a file is moved, the document is often lost entirely.

A global scheme of unique identifiers is required, one that has persistence beyond the life of the originating organization and that is not tied to specific locations or processes. These names must remain valid whenever documents are moved from one location to another, or are migrated from one storage medium to another.

Three examples of schemes proposed to get around the problem of persistent naming are PURLs, URNs, and Digital Object Identifiers.

PURLS : PURLs are persistent URLs. They are a scheme developed by OCLC in an attempt to separate a document name from its location and therefore increase the probability that it will always be found. PURLs work through a mapping of a unique, never-changing PURL to an actual URL. If a document moves, the URL is updated, but the PURL stays the same. In operation, a user requests a document through a PURL, a PURL server looks up the corresponding URL in a database, and then the URL is used to pass the document to the user. Because PURLs also confound a name with an access method, like URLs, they are not true names (Lynch, 1998).

Uniform Resource Name (URN) : URNs are a

development of the Internet Engineering Task Force (IETF). A URN is not a naming scheme in itself, but a framework for defining identifiers (Lynch, 1998). They contain a naming authority identifier (a central authority given the task of assigning identifiers) and an object identifier (assigned by the central authority). Like PURLs, URNs must be resolved, through a database or other such system, into actual URLs. Unlike PURLs, however, a URN can be resolved into more than one URL, such as one for each of several different formats. There is currently no working URN system.

Digital Object Identifier (DOI) System : DOI is an initiative by the Association of American Publishers and the (American) Corporation for National Research Initiatives designed to provide a method by which digital objects can be reliably identified and accessed. The CNRI Handle system, which underlies DOI, is a system that resolves digital identifiers into the information required to locate and access a digital object. The main impetus of the DOI system is to provide publishers with a method by which the intellectual property right issues associated with their materials can be managed.

The issue of persistent naming raises it head in a coordinated scheme, as well. Persistent names are an organizational problem, rather than an engineering problem. Technically, a system to handle names is possible, however, unique identifiers will only persist if some institution takes responsibility for their management and migration from a current technology to succeeding generations of technologies. Thus, one goal of a coordinated digital library scheme would be to identify an institution or institutions that would take charge of issuing, resolving, and migrating a system of unique names.

6. Copyright / rights management : Copyright has been called the "single most vexing barrier to digital library development" (Chepesuik, 1997:49). The current paper-based concept of copyright breaks down in the digital environment because the control of copies is lost. Digital objects are less fixed, easily copied, and remotely accessible by multiple users simultaneously. The problem for libraries is that, unlike private businesses or publishers that own their information, libraries are, for the most part, simply caretakers of information they don't own the copyright of the material they hold. It is unlikely that libraries will ever be able to freely digitize and provide access to the copyrighted materials in their collections. Instead, they will have to develop mechanisms for managing copyright, mechanisms that allow them to provide information without violating copyright, called rights management.

Some rights management functions could include, for example:

- usage tracking
- identifying and authenticating users
- providing the copyright status of each digital object, and the restrictions on its use or the fees associated with it
- handling transactions with users by allowing only so many copies to be accessed, or by charging them for a copy, or by passing the request on to a publisher

7. Preservation : Another important issue is preservation¾ keeping digital information available in perpetuity. In the preservation of digital materials, the real issue is technical obsolescence. Technical obsolescence in the digital age is like the deterioration of paper in the paper age. Libraries in the pre-digital era had to worry about climate control and the de-acidification of books, but the preservation of digital information will mean constantly coming up with new technical solutions.

When considering digital materials, there are three types of "preservation" one can refer to:

The preservation of the storage medium : Tapes, hard drives, and floppy discs have a very short life span when considered in terms of obsolescence. The data on them can be refreshed, keeping the bits valid, but refreshing is only effective as long as the media are still current. The media used to store digital materials become obsolete in anywhere from two to five years before they are replaced by better technology. Over the long term, materials stored on older media could be lost because there will no longer have the hardware or software to read them. Thus, libraries will have to keep moving digital information from storage medium to storage medium.

The preservation of access to content : This form of preservation involves preserving access to the content of documents, regardless of their format. While files can be moved from one physical storage medium to another, what happens when the formats (e.g., Adobe Acrobat PDF) containing the information become obsolete? This is a problem perhaps bigger than that of obsolete storage technologies. One solution is to do data migration¾ that is, translate data from one format to another preserving the ability of users to retrieve and display the information content. However, there are difficulties here too— data migration is costly, there are as yet no standards for data migration, and distortion or information loss is inevitably introduced every time data is migrated from format to format.

The bottom line is that no one really knows how yet how to best migrate digital information. Preserving digital information: The Report of the Task Force on Archiving of Digital Information (RLG, 1995) by the US Commission on Preservation and Access and RLG states, "the preservation community is only beginning to address migration of complex digital objects" and such migration remains "largely experimental." Even if there were adequate technology available today, information will have to be migrated from format to format over many generations, passing a huge and costly responsibility to those who come after.

The preservation of fixed-media materials through digital technology : This slant on the issue involves the use of digital technology as a replacement for current preservation media, such as microforms. Again, there are, as yet, no common standards for the use of digital media as a preservation medium and it is unclear whether digital media are as yet up to the task of long-term preservation. Digital preservation standards will be required to consistently store and share materials preserved digitally (Chepesuik, 1997).

What can libraries jointly do in a coordinated scheme? They can:

- create policies for long-term preservation
- ensure that redundant permanent copies are stored at designated institutions
- help establish preservation standards to consistently store and share materials preserved digitally

CURRENT TRENDS IN DIGITAL LIBRARY

Library and Information science being a discipline has had the trend of adopting innovative practices which aids in effectiveness and efficiency of the services. Transcending from semi digital libraries to total digital libraries will be inevitable in the 21'century. Some of the emerging trends that will impact libraries and librarianship in a big way are presented here.

Total multimedia solution will be accessible to a large number of institutions as there will be improvement in streaming technologies, and network bandwidth will be more economical. Accepted standards will be incorporated by software vendors as they eye the library market which is at present in the discussion phase and the experimental stage of trying the standards. A successful trend would be the transition of digital libraries from being computer science experiments to being major library implementations. (Sujin, 2013)

Many faculty members of leading universities are managing their teaching through course specific web pages like Blackboard and Web CT wherein necessary support facilities like online discussion forums, automatic grading, etc are provided. But the concern as expressed by David Seaman in his paper 'Aggregation, Integration, and Openness: Current Trends in Digital Libraries, such courseware systems are often installed and run by IT departments without much library involvement and there is little human and technical interface between the library content management systems and the courseware systems. Also there is difficulty in linking the webpage course contents to the holdings of the digital library supporting it. He has further observed that 'the advent of courseware holds great promise for moving the library into the classroom but so far the reality falls short of this opportunity to engage even more richly with the work of our teachers and students'. (Seaman, David DLF.USA http://www.dlf.org) So this trend prompts us to have more of library involvement in course design and delivery for effective output.

CONCLUSION

Libraries around the world have been working on this daunting set of challenges for several years now. The library/information center has to overcome the inhibitions and look ahead for the betterment of information services to the user community by successfully adopting the digital technology - the need of the hour and keep pace with world. Information technology has changed the world and has become one important tool for retrieving information new days. Library collections are not only limited to printed documents but also electronic resources increases by their use and therefore it is important to develop digital library. It seems that the days may not far when the whole world would have digital libraries interconnecting all libraries to meet the academic and research needs within the short time. However, before digital libraries took over the library and information network, the country's archives laws needs to be changed to meet the current challenges in the areas of copyright protection of data and prevention of corruption of data.

QUESTIONS

1. Define how libraries transition from traditional to digital?
2. List the characteristics of digital libraries?
3. Define Merits and demerits of digital libraries?
4. What the challenges faced by digital libraries?

2

Digital Library Management

INTRODUCTION

The terms, electronic library, digital library and virtual library have been used interchangeably and now widely accepted as a description of the use of digital technology by libraries to acquire, store, conserve and make available their content to remote users.

The term digital library was best defined by Christine Borgaman as 'a set of electronic resources and associated technological capabilities for creating searching and using information... they are an extension and enhancement of information storage and retrieval systems that manipulate data in any medium... The content of digital libraries includes data [and] metadata'.

In a broad sense, a digital library may be treated as an organized and managed collection of highly quality information content in a variety of media (text, still image, moving image, sound or combination thereof), but all in digital forms, accessible over different electronic networks.

Such a digital library includes a number of search or navigation aids that both operate within that particular library and allow access to other collection of information connected by networks worldwide.

OBJECTIVES

- Impact knowlegde on interoperability and data exchange in digital libraries and roles of standrards and protocols
- Introduction to standards and protocols and their need and importance in digital libraries
- Digital library design models and architecture with examples of digital libraries built using these models

MANAGING DIGITAL LIBRARY

In a digital library are organized and managed for the purpose of immediate access to the target audience. How contents are developed and managed, is a critical issue to the long term success of digital library services, especially when technical resources are limited.

Management includes the following key functions:

- Selection and acquisition;
- Indexing;
- Storage;
- Retrieval;
- Maintenance; and
- Rights management.

Selection and Acquisition

Libraries select content according to a well-defined collection development policy. Such policy manifests the mission of a library and determines how budgets on materials expended. There are two key challenges in content selection i.e. cost and quality. Firstly, librarian should consider the cost of acquisition. Intellectual property rights are important considerations, but the cost of digitization and maintenance must also be taken into account. Secondly, librarian should consider the quality of the content before acquiring it. This is more problematic consideration because issue of authorities as well as veracity arises. As soon as decision about selection is made, content must be acquired. For objects, which are already in digital form, the file transfer through networks or mass storage is straightforward and as long as file formats are well specified. In case of traditional objects, digitization must be done. Scanners for text and images range in quality on several dimensions (i.e. output resolution, value and conditions of physical objects and speed) are required. In addition to these technical challenges policy decision must be made. For example, which resolution and formats to adopt, which text to OCR subsequently error correct, how to link different representation for multiple media from single collections.

Indexing

Once content has been selected and acquired, it will be added to the collection in such a way that users may retrieve it easily. And thus, indexing is required for digital content to search and access in a selective way like OPAC for printed content. Decisions are to be taken regarding what to be indexed (author, keywords, phrase, etc), how the content and index files are linked, what sort of access points are provided, etc. Indexing strategy comprises not only of what types of fields are to be indexed, but how they are to be treated (exhaustive or sparse). Automatic indexing techniques are used to index the content of digital library. Texts are indexed using vector-space or probabilistic information retrieval models that provide access through weighted values for all but a few cornmon words, and thus the classification system itself is empirically determined from the data as a by-product of the indexing. Inquiry system is the most successful example of this approach used as the retrieval engine in many digital library projects (e.g., Library of congress). These approaches based on traditional approach of manually assigning object to a limited number of manually constructed concept classes (classification system) represented in a control vocabulary (e.g., Library of Congress subject headings or medical subject headings). Other automatic techniques index object to mathematically abstract concept classes. Several www-based services use a hybrid approach by manually creating classification system and then using automatic techniques to assign objects. Most retrieval systems for images, video, audio recordings and other non-textual objects have depended on text items such as title, creator name or manually assigned subject headings for retrieval. It seems certain that digital library research and development activity of 1990s will ensure that considerable progress is made in automatic indexing for textual and non-textual objects. New indexing challenges will emerge as more dynamic objects (e.g., virtual conference proceeding, active networks) are added to digital libraries. The temporal nature of such objects will require on-going indexing techniques.

Storage

The next thing is how to store the content of digital library. Decisions regarding procuring suitable hardware, software, networking, etc. are to be made at this stage. Storage is mainly a technical requirement, although new media may complicate storage decision and costing. When data are to deliver continuously (e.g., streaming video or audio) rather than as discrete files, alternative technologies are required. Drives and database management software that operate continuously have different engineering requirements from drives optimized for bursts of data. Large digital repositories are required multiple level of mass storage media (e.g., disk, tape, etc.) and mechanical robots to locate and mounts the media. Various supercomputer centers are using tape robots that store and access to many terabytes of data. Digital libraries will surely apply such technology just as libraries of today apply movable shelving and complex conveyer systems to move physical materials.

Retrieval

Retrieval is another major issue, as far as digital library content and its access is concerned. Ultimately, users must be able to retrieve the content, which have been selected, indexed and stored by the librarians. During 1970s to 1980s, a large number of libraries invested heavily in computerizing cataloging and circulation functions to give users better access and services. Online Public Access Catalogues (OPACs) have long provided author, title, and limited subject access to local holdings (and more recently to union holdings across to multiple libraries). The expectation for digital collection is that catalogue should seamlessly link to the digital content itself so that remotely located users can find and display not only bibliographic records, but also primary information objects. In physical libraries, the card catalogues or OPAC is physically distinct from the items on shelves. These distinctions are difficult to make in electronic environments because everything is displayed on the same physical screen and thus, the boundaries between metadata and primary data are often blurred. Distinguishing metadata and primary data is not a trivial problem in rich collections. In homogenous collections it is possible to define a unit of primary content (e.g., a book rather than a character or series), but this is more problematic in heterogeneous collections containing findings aids, manuscripts, bitmaps, videos and hypertexts. Expectation to provide primary data with metadata yields several challenges to librarians. The challenges are first to extract and provide multiple levels of representation and second to provide user with control mechanisms to move from high-level surrogates to detailed objects. Huge challenges remain in creating surrogates for digital content. Today most retrieval is facilitated through words, titles, captions, manually created subscriptions, automatically extracted keywords and so on. There is enormous attention focused on creating non textual surrogates such as colour and shape characterizations for images and speaker identification schemes for audio recordings, but there are more difficult metadata issues looming as more contents are not stored at all but created on the fly according to the specifications of the users.

Today digital libraries offer access to primary content using a variety of access tools. An active area of research is user interfaces for digital collections. Access interfaces depend on the content organization and storage and serve as the bridge between internal (technical services) and user services.

Maintenance

Maintaining buildings and systems and preserving content are important and costly activities in physical libraries. Digital libraries may avoid some of the cost of wear and tear on buildings and books but still have significant maintenance costs, including some unique to electronic environments. New equipment, improved or alternative networks solutions (e.g. ISDN, ATM, Wireless), and software upgrades will require excellent technical personnel. Archivists have long worried about the persistence of digital media. Magnetic tape life expectancies are typically less than ten years under ideal temperature and humidity conditions. Optical storage offers longer life spans, but digital librarians must plan for copying digital holdings periodically and specially for the inevitable obsolescences of different media types and playback devices. These maintenance issues correspond to traditional maintenance requirements, but they apply across many industries and require rapidly changing technical skills, which tend to be much expensive.

Just as the computational system change, digital content may also change. A digital document may have numerous versions, especially given the ease with which electronic documents may have changed. Maintaining the most essential document requires that versions be well managed, which includes updating and deleting the links to those objects [10]. In addition to this version control problem, digital librarians must manage the multiplicity of indexes and file formats. Requirements for link managements are more problematic, as hypertext links are created among distinct documents. Although much research and development efforts in digital libraries have been devoted to maintaining the content, but further improvements are required to maintain security, updating versions, tools for automatically checking links, database tools for property rights, etc. for the smooth library functions and services.

Rights Management

Intellectual property right and information security and authority are two global interdependent issues, which influence research and development in digital libraries. Copyright exists to promote intellectual production by providing economic incentives. Security protects unauthorized access as well as ensures the veracity and authority of digital information objects. The misuse that can be put to digital content is far more serious and voluminous than for printed content. There are various legal issues that make management difficult for digital content. The legal and related issues include: what does it mean to use intellectual property; how can its fair use apply to digital objects; how and whether it may be represented in machine readable form; how, by whom and in what conditions it may be used; how it protects against illegal use, etc.

The efforts have been made to change copy right laws to protect the illegal use of digital objects. And also to develop technical solutions that protects copyright either through copy protection or automatic billing mechanism. Research on encryption algorithms, digital watermarking and electronic commerce are leading to the development of trusted system that protect intellectual property rights by managing the necessary financial transactions while protecting consumers by providing authoritative information securely. These techniques ensure the veracity of an object and may help to prevent copying and distribution in an open marketplace.

DESIGN AND ORGANIZATION OF DIGITAL LIBRARIES DEVELOPMENT OF DIGITAL LIBRARIES

Some of the important points to be considered in developing a digital library are

1. Digital collection or material selection
2. Conversion of existing Print, Audio and video into digital format.
3. Cataloguing or Metadata creation
4. Storing
5. Creating portals or gateway to the electronic collection available on the web
6. Integrated access interface.

Digital Collection

One of the important issues in the creation of a digital library is the building up of a digital collection. A digital library can have a wide range of resources. It can obtain both conventional documents and / or digital or computer processible form. The conversion of digital form is just to ensure better access and to reduce dependence on physical libraries.

The new digital resources are either deliberately created as digital or created in parallel to print. Publishers are increasingly moving to XML or SGML format. Future digital libraries resources are electronic journals, electronic books through databases and datasets in many formats.

The acquisitions of documents, which are already available in digital formats, like CD-ROM database is a part of the transition . Nowadays a large number of information products are available on CD-ROM, like MEDLINE, COMPENDEX, METADEX, LISA etc. Libraries can subscribe to any of these database for providing bibliographic or full text information forms an important input to the digital collection.

Access to external digital collection

Digital libraries can acquire permission to digital collections provided by external sources like other institutions, commercial publishers, resources of other libraries, and electronic journals through on-line access. Many of the commercial publishers like Elsevier, Academic press, ACM, SIAM are making their journals available on-line through web sites. Many of the journals are available in print and as well as in electronic form.

Conversion of existing Print, Audio and Video into digital format

Nowadays, a part of conventional collection of a library is being converted into digital form. The process of conversion of paper documents into digital format is mainly with the help of scanners. Printed text, pictures and figures are transformed into computer accessible forms using a digital scanner or a digital camera.

Scanners are mostly using for converting print resources into digital format. Most scanning software generate by default TIFF (Tagged Image File Format). The scanned textual images (TIF) are not searchable nor can be manipulated like text file document (ASCII). The scanned TIF format is converted to text by the process of

Optical Character Recognition (OCR). The OCR software allows the option of maintaining text and graphics in their original layout as well as plain ASCII and word processing formats. Through OCR software we can save the file into html, doc and other formats. The images can be browsed through a table of contents composed in HTML providing linked to scanned images.

The important step involved in the process of digitization is scanning, as explained above with the help of scanners. Some of the important scanners being used for capturing digital images are

(a) Minolta PS 7000

(b) HP scanjet 6,300 C,

(c) Bell and Howell 1000 FB,

(d) Kodak 500s

(e) Digital camera - Zentschel omini scan 3000 Minolta PS 3000,

(f) Slide scanner - Kodak PCD Scanner 4045

(g) Microfilm scanner - Mekel M 500 XL sunrise SRI - 150

Some of the image scanning software is

Quick Scan

Altris software

OPTM Documentum

File net

Java system

Power office

Caere's Omni page

ABBYY

Fine reader

Storing

Digital resources can be stored in CD, DVD, Tape and Hard disk. Usually the things to be digitize will be in

Image, Text, Audio and Video. The Text, Image and Photographs after scanning is stored in the in JPEG (Joint Photographic Experts Groups) and GIF (Graphics Interchange Format). These two formats are widely used for storage Images because they are small, fast and capable of displaying any type of picture. Audio files can be saved in .wav, .mp3, midi etc format. Recently developed MP3 format is very compact and takes less space while quality of audio is also better compared to other formats. The digitized View files are saved in .mov or .avi, divx, mpeg file formats.

Access to digital information availability on web

The web provides the hyper media based systems that allow rapid access to a wide variety of networked information resources. One can browse the different web sites which are scattered geographically and have access to the major resources from which one can download the information.

So digital libraries can develop their collection through the integration of a number of resources and media types. Digital libraries can also provide access to electronic resources through library home pages.

DIGITAL LIBRARY DESIGN

The following aspects can be considered as guidelines for the development of the digital library architecture.

Service driven : The architecture for the digital library must be driven by the services it provides and tools required for delivering the service.

Open Architecture : The architecture of the digital library must be open, extensible and support interoperability among heterogeneous, distributed systems.

Scalability : The digital library architecture must be robust, scalable and reliable with high transaction rate for users with a wide variety of backgrounds and information needs.

Practicality : The digital library architecture should represent a flexible and practical approach to standards, recognizing the need to balance the level of information collection with economic constraints.

Privacy : The digital library architecture must be sensitive to privacy issues and support both anonymous and customized access to resources.

Time Frame : The time frame required to plan for system migration in the next year as well as planning for a technology generation framework should be approximately 3 to 5 years.

DIGITAL LIBRARY ARCHITECTURE

Major problems of digital library design are caused by differences in the computer systems, file structure, formats, information organization and different information retrieval requirements of collections (such e-journals, e-books, reference sources, online courseware, GIS, etc.) accessible through the digital library. While the web has emerged as the preferred media of information delivery and access, the use of standards and protocols makes it possible to make digital collections interoperable and accessible seamlessly. Some of the important features that should be considered while designing a digital library architecture are as follows:

Open Architecture : Open architecture refers to computer architecture or software architecture that allows adding, upgrading and swapping components or software modules. As opposed to open architecture, software and hardware with closed architecture have pre-defined modules or components that are not generally upgradable.

Open architecture allows potential users to see inside all or parts of the architecture without any proprietary constraints. Typically, an open architecture publishes all or parts of its architecture that the developer or integrator wants to share. Digital library design should use open architecture and a set of well-defined standards and protocols so as to facilitate scalability and interoperability.

Scalability, Extensibility and Sustainability : The scalability, extensibility and sustainability are three most important design features of a digital library that addresses the issue of the ability of a digital library to handle the increased volume of digital objects and its ability to sustain it for a long period of time. The digital library design should ensure that software should be able to handle large quantity of data, and hardware and network should be scalable to handle large quantity of digital objects and its transmission over the network. Moreover, digital library design and planning should provide for human and financial resources required for sustaining the digital library on long-term basis.

Seamless Access : The digital libraries should provide transparent, seamless and platform-independent access to distributed array of information resources to users.

Interoperability : Interoperability addresses the issue of ability of digital libraries and its components to work together effectively in order to exchange information in a useful and meaningful manner. Use of open architecture and a set of well-defined standards and protocols ensure interoperability amongst heterogeneous digital libraries in a distributed environment.

Federation : Federation refers to distribution of responsibilities for content creation, management and administration of various functions and service of digital libraries. It needs to be ensured that the participants follow the agreed standards, technologies and tools.

Digital Preservation : The architecture of the digital library must ensure persistent and long-term access to its collection.

Modularity : It is a design approach that adheres to four fundamental tenets of cohesiveness, encapsulation, self-containment and high binding to design a system component as an independently operable unit.

Platform Independence : The digital library architecture should be platform- independent both at hardware and software level.

Multiplicity of Files & Formats : Digital library should be able to handle multiple files and formats such as unstructured / structured text, audio, video, images, graphics, animation, etc

Location-independent Identifiers : Digital objects in the digital library should support location-independent identifiers such as handles, PURLs, DOI and OpenURL.

DIGITAL LIBRARY ARCHITECTURE AND DESIGN

Different digital libraries have their own underlying design and architecture. Most digital library architectures provide for the five key components

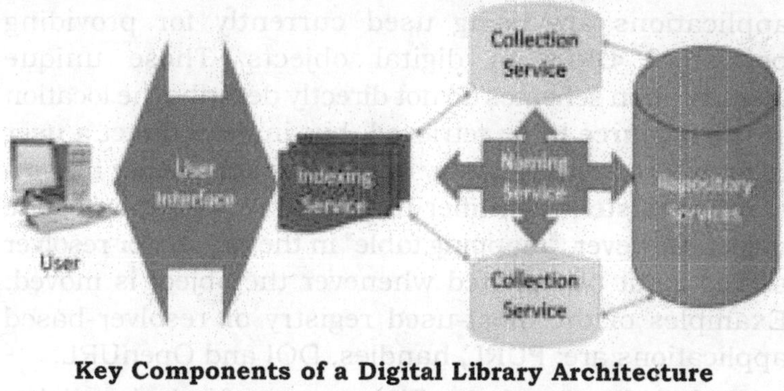

Key Components of a Digital Library Architecture

1. User Interfaces : Digital libraries are required to provide interfaces for the user facilitating them to explore its collection, conduct searches, navigate through hierarchical menus of subjects, select and deselect searchable options, and sort search results in a fashion required by them.

2. Digital Repository : Digital repositories store and manage digital objects and metadata. The digital objects in a digital library may be "born digital" or digitized from the legacy document through the process of scanning. The metadata, that describes the digital objects to facilitate searching and discovery, may be extracted automatically or created manually. A large digital library may have several distributed repositories depending on collections it holds. The digital library developers interface with digital repository using Repository Access Protocol (RAP). RAP recognizes rights and permissions to enforce intellectual property rights, if required. E-commerce functionalities may also be present, if needed to handle accounting and billing.

3. Digital Objects Naming Service: Unique Identifiers : Digital objects in a repository require location-independent unique identifiers. These identifiers must remain valid whenever documents are moved from one location to another, or are migrated from one storage medium to another. A number of registry or resolver-based applications are being used currently for providing persistent URLs to digital objects. These unique identification schemes do not directly describe the location of the resource to be retrieved, but instead direct a user to an intermediate registry or resolver server that maps a static persistent identifier to the current location of the object. However, "mapping table" in the registry or resolver server must be updated whenever the object is moved. Examples of the most-used registry or resolver-based applications are: PURL, handles, DOI and OpenURL.

4. Index Services : The process of indexing digital objects involves linking of database of digital objects to a text database consisting of keywords and subject descriptors. Digital objects are required to be linked to the associated keywords and subject descriptors so as to facilitate their retrieval. A digital repository typically stores a large amount of unstructured data in a two file system for storing and retrieving digital objects. The first file stores keywords or descriptors of digital objects along with a key to a second file. The second file contains the location of digital objects. The user selects a record from the first file using a search algorithm. Once the user selects a keyword or a descriptor from the first file, the location index in the second file finds the digital object and displays it. It is assumed that a digital repository has several indices and catalogues that can be searched to discover information for subsequent retrieval from a repository.

5. Search System and Content Delivery : The design of the digital library system should support searching of its collection. The search engine should support features like Boolean searching, proximity searching, phrase searching, etc. that are supported by the traditional information retrieval system. Most digital library software integrates external search engines. Dspace, for example, uses the Apache Lucene search engine. The digital library should also support content delivery via file transfer or streaming media.

STANDARDS AND PROTOCOLS

Standards and protocols are the backbone of a digital library that is instrumental in its efficient implementation with utmost quality and consistency facilitating interoperability, data transfer and exchange of the system. Uniform standards and protocols are pre-requisite for data transfer, exchange and interoperability amongst digital libraries.

A protocol is a series of prescribed steps to be taken, usually in order to allow for the coordinated action of multiple parties. In the world of computers, protocols are used to allow different computers and/or software applications to work and communicate with one another. Because computer protocols are frequently formalized by national and international standard organizations such as ISO and ITU, they are also considered as standards.

As such, a protocol that is accepted by most of the parties that implement it can be considered as standard. However, every protocol is not a standard, likewise every standard is not a protocol. Standards are generally agreed-upon models for comparison. In the world of computers, standards are often used to define syntactic or other rule sets, and occasionally protocols, that are used as a basis for comparison. (Ascher Interactive, 2007).

Standards support cooperative relationships amongst multiple vendors and implementors and provide a common base from which individual developments may emerge. Standards make it possible to share and collaborate in developments of products and processes across institutional and political boundaries. Moreover, too many standards for the same products and processes undermine the utility of having any standard at all. Standard for citing bibliographic references is a good example since there are numerous rival and incompatible standards that are used to citing a document, for example the American Psychological Association, the Modern Language Association, the Chicago Manual of Style, Indian standards, ANSI Z39.29 (American National Standard for Bibliographic References) and several other well-known standards that can be used by editors or publishers as their standard.

Standards are supported by a range of national and international organizations, including professional associations such as the Institute of Electrical and Electronics Engineers (IEEE), national standard institutions such as the American National Standards Institute (ANSI) or the British Standards Institution (BSI) or Bureau of Indian Standards, and international bodies such as the International Organization for Standardization (ISO). The US National Information Standards Organization (NISO), accredited by ANSI is specifically assigned the task of preparing standards for library and information science.

A number of important institutions and organizations are actively involved in the development and promotion of standards relevant to digital libraries. For example, the Digital Library Federation (DLF), a consortium of libraries and related agencies, as one of its objectives identify standards for digital collections and network access (http://www.diglib.org). The DLF operates under the administrative umbrella of the Council of Library and Information Resources (http://www.clir.org) located in Washington, DC. The Library of Congress (http://www.loc.gov), plays an important role in maintaining several key standards such as MARC, and the development of MARC within an XML environment. The International Federation of Library Associations and Institutions (IFLA) maintains a gateway– IFLANET Digital Libraries – to resources about a variety of relevant standards

COMMUNICATION PROTOCOLS

Communication protocols are predefined sets of prompts and responses which two computers follow while communicating with each other. Since digital libraries are designed around Internet and Web technologies, communication protocols such as Transmission Control Protocol / Internet Protocol (TCP/IP), Hyper Text Transfer Protocol (http) and File Transfer Protocol (ftp) that are used by the Internet are also used for establishing communication between clients and servers in a digital library.

1. Transmission Control Protocol / Internet Protocol (TCP/IP) : The Internet is a packet-switched network, wherein information to be communicated, is broken down into small packets. These packets are sent individually using several different routes at the same time and then reassembled at the receiving end. TCP is the component that collects and reassembles the packets of data, while IP is responsible for assuring that the packets are sent to the right destination. TCP/IP was developed in the 1970s and adopted as the protocol standard for ARPANET, the predecessor to the Internet, in 1983.

TCP/IP is the protocol that controls the creation of transmission paths between computers on a single network as well as between different networks. The standard defines how electronic devices (like computers) should be connected to the Internet, and how data should be transmitted between them. This protocol is used universally for public networks and many in-house local area networks. Originally designed for the UNIX operating system, TCP/IP software is now available for every major kind of computer operating system and is a de facto standard for transmitting data over networks.

Moreover, the TCP/IP includes commands and facilities that facilitates transfer of files between systems, log in to remote systems, run commands on remote systems, print files on remote systems, send electronic mail to remote users, converse interactively with remote users, manage a network, etc. Fig. 1 and Fig. 2 given below is pictorial depiction of TCP / IP model.

2. Hyper Text Transfer Protocol (http) : The http is the underlying protocol used by the WWW to define how messages are formatted and transmitted. It needs an http client program (Internet Browser) on one end, and an http server program on the other end. The protocol is used for carrying requests from clients to the server and returning pages to the client. It is also used for sending requests from one server to another. Http is the most important protocol used in the World Wide Web (WWW).

HTTP runs on top of the TCP/IP protocol. Web browsers are HTTP clients that send file requests to Web servers, which, in turn, handle the requests via an HTTP service. HTTP was originally proposed in 1989 by Tim Berners-Lee, who was a coauthor of the 1.0 specification of http. HTTP, in its 1.0 version was "stateless", i.e. each new request from a client required setting-up of a new connection instead of handling all requests from the same client through the same connection. Moreover, the version 1.0 of the protocol provided for raw data transfer across the Internet. However, version 1.1 was an improved protocol that included persistent connections, decompression of HTML files by client browsers, multiple domain names sharing the same IP address and handling MIME-like messages. Fig. 3 is pictorial depiction of client-server Interaction using http protocol.

File Transfer Protocol (FTP)

The File Transfer Protocol (FTP), as its name indicate, is a protocol for transferring files from one computer to another over a local area network (LAN) or a wide area network (WAN) such as Internet. It is a common method of moving files between between client and server over TCP / IP network. The protocol is in existence since 1971 when the file transfer system was first implemented between MIT machines. FTP provides for reliable and swift exchange of files with different operating system and machine architecture. There are many Internet sites that have established publicly accessible repositories of material that can be obtained using FTP, by logging in using the account name anonymous, thus these sites are called anonymous ftp servers. Fig. 4 is pictorial depiction of FTP process model.

Bibliographic Standards

Bibliographic standards are concerned with the description of contents as well as physical attributes of documents and non-documents in a library. They are generally very complex (MARC has some 700 field definitions) and cover the most difficult and intellectual part of the object definition (Day, 2001) . These definitions are necessary for processing the material and also for searching it. Most digital libraries software support Dublin Core Metadata Sets for bibliographic records.

1. Machine Readable Catalogue (MARC) : MARC (MAchine-Readable Cataloging) standards are a set of formats for description of documents catalogued by libraries including books, journals, conference proceedings, CD ROM, etc. 'Machine-readable' essentially means that a computer can read and interpret the data given in the cataloging record. MARC was developed in 1960s by the US Library of Congress to create records that can be used by computers and shared among libraries. MARC contains bibliographic elements for content, physical and process description. By 1971, MARC formats had become the US national standard and international standard by 1973. There are several versions of MARC in use around the world, the most predominant being MARC 21, created in 1999 as a result of the harmonization of U.S. and Canadian MARC formats, and UNIMARC, widely used in Europe. The MARC 21 family of standards now includes formats for authority records, holdings records, classification schedules, and community information, in addition to the format for bibliographic records (Furrie, 2003).

2. Dublin Core : The Dublin Core refers to a set of metadata element that may be assigned to web pages so as to facilitate discovery of electronic resources. Originally conceived for author-generated description of web resources at the OCLC/NCSA Metadata Workshop held at Dublin, Ohio in 1995, it has attracted the attention of formal resource description communities such as museums, libraries, government agencies, and commercial organizations. The Dublin Core Workshop Series has gathered experts from the library world, the networking and digital library research communities, and a variety of content specialists in a series of invitational workshops. The building of an interdisciplinary, international consensus around a core element set is the central feature of the Dublin Core. A set of 15 core elements in Dublin Core include: Title, Creator, Subject and Keywords,

Description, Publisher, Contributor, Date, Resource Type, Format, Resource Identifier, Source, Language, Relation, Coverage, Rights Management. (Baker, 1998).

3. BIB-1 : BIB-1 is a simplified record structure for online transmission. It is essentially a sub-set of MARC. It is the original format for transmission of records within a Z39.50 dialogue between two systems. It has elements that are mappable to both MARC and the Dublin Core (Library of Congress, 2007).

4. Text Encoding Initiative (TEI) : The initiative provides a scheme for encoded text so that parts of it such as the start and end of lines, paragraph, pages, chapters, acts, and so on can be marked. Thus such text can be processed to produce accurate indexes for searching. Other features of the text both grammatical and linguistic and also content indicating such as the actors in a play can be identified allowing for a rich analysis. These rules require that the actual text be marked up with SGML encoding (TEI, 2013).

5. Electronic Archival Description (EAD) : An encoding scheme devised within the SGML framework to define the content description of documents and other archival objects. It is defined with a minimum number of descriptive elements, but in an extensible fashion. It is designed to create descriptive records which will assist in searching for the original material in a number of ways (Library of Congress, 2007).

6. Metadata Encoding and Transmission Standard (METS) : METS has the task of encoding descriptive, administrative and structural metadata for objects in a digital library to facilitate the management of such documents within a repository and their exchange between repositories. It is maintained by the Network Development and MARC Standards Office of the Library of Congress and is an initiative of the Digital Library Federation, mentioned earlier in the Chapter (Library of Congress, 2013). The METS format has seven major sections:

i. The METS Header contains metadata describing the METS document itself, including such information as creator or editor.

ii. The Descriptive Metadata section points to descriptive metadata external to the METS document (such as a MARC record in an OPAC or an EAD finding aid on a web server), or contain internally embedded descriptive metadata, or both.

iii. The Administrative Metadata section provides information about how the files were created and stored, intellectual property rights, the original source from which the digital library object document derives, and information regarding the provenance of the files comprising the digital library object (that is master/derivative file relationships, and migration / transformation information). As with Descriptive Metadata, Administrative Metadata may be either external to the METS document, or encoded internally.

iv. The File section lists all the files containing content that form part of the digital document.

v. The Structural Map provides a hierarchical structure for the digital library document or object, and links the elements of that structure to content files and metadata that pertain to each element.

vi. The Structural Links section of METS allows METS' creators to record the existence of hyperlinks between nodes in the hierarchy outlined in the Structural Map. This is of particular value when using METS to archive websites.

vii. The Behaviour section associates executable behaviours with content in the document.

7. Metadata Object Description Schema (MODS): The Metadata Object Description Schema was developed as a descriptive metadata scheme oriented toward digital objects, and drawing from the MAchine Readable

Cataloging (MARC 21) Format. The scheme is reasonably usable, fairly refined as it provides descriptive metadata for digital objects by regrouping the MARC fields, adding a few new ones, and translating the numeric codes to readable English in XML.

MODS has gone through intense development, version 3.1 was released 27 July 2005, and version 3.2 was released 1 June 2006. In addition, MODS was adopted by the Digital Library Federation (DLF) for their Aquifer Project which is seeking to develop the best possible methods and services for federated access to digital resources. DLF intends to use MODS to replace Dublin Core for descriptive metadata for digital objects in the digital library world, for MODS allows more specification of contents and better clarification of the various elements than does Dublin Core (Library of Congress, 2013).

INTEROPERABILITY: NECESSITIES

As noted earlier, the emergence of need to interoperable DLs is obviously tangible, so that users could simply search a library or database and obtain their required content. OCLC is an example of such an interoperable system. Its product, WorldCat, was established more than 20 years ago and is still in use. WorldCat's collection covers a large shared list of bibliographic data in the world (Spies, 2001). So OCLC established a system in which libraries all over the world share their bibliographic data on the WorldCat context. Almost 15 years ago, Lynch and Garcia-Molina (1995) in a workshop in the USA expressed that the key challenges in DL research are:

- interoperability;
- description of objects and repositories;
- collection management and organization;
- user interfaces; and
- human-computer interaction.

This was subsequently noted by Warren and Alsmeyer (2005) showing that interoperability is one of the most heavily discussed issues in DL research. The requirement for interoperability generally derives from the fact that various DLs with different architectures, metadata formats, and underlying technologies wish to effectively interact, something they can do through applying a range of common protocols and standards (Shiri, 2003).

Consequently, there are many reasons so as to discuss about interoperability in DLs. We mentioned some of them in this section in order to show its necessities for libraries, especially for DLs.

Interoperability models Interoperability between digital archives is applicable by three different models as mentioned above. Each digital archive uses diverse technology and tools that is related to the time of developing, the amount of money that developers want to expend, and also the efficiency that the developers expect. Altogether digital libraries that want to offer integrated services in cooperating with other libraries, often encounter with methods that are appropriate for their users. Also, there are generally accepted standards, in this way, which are less efficient. Sometimes a new method provides more effectiveness for a digital library, but fewer users could use it. For instance, simple tags such as hyper text markup language (HTML) and public protocols like hyper text transfer protocol (HTTP) could be used which are accessible for everyone in the world. Furthermore, digital libraries could use the last version of Java applets related technology in HTML. These applicants could be useful for users that have high-speed networks and use modern search engines. Hence, users that do not have such applicants could not use them.

In fact, the act of removing tension between performance, cost and technology has a direct relation to content and users. Sometimes, it is better to choose simple technology and offer comprehensive but superficial services. At the other time, it is logical to choose high performance technology with high cost. Certainly, just high-motivated digital libraries use these high cost methods which of course, are successive in contrast. Consequently, the above-mentioned items promote diverse methods for interoperability. As expressed above, there are three basic models of interoperability:

(1) federated; (2) harvesting, and (3) gathering. The first one provides the strongest form of interoperability, but places the greatest burden on participants. The last one requires essentially no effort by the participants, but provides a poorer level of interoperability. And the middle one is the average of the others (Arms et al., 2002). These three models of performing interoperability are all employed in digital libraries, and also there are factually various performing methods in each model. In addition, there are applications that use a combination of the models or even use all of them in their projects. In this sense, they use, for instance, Z39.50 and OAI in order to make access to some of the collections. As will be discussed in this section, each one is related to different model. In this section, the studied projects and researches are presented in this framework chronologically, three models of performing interoperability.

1. Federated model : "Federation can be considered the conventional approach to interoperability. In federation, a group of organizations agree that their services will conform to certain specifications, which are often selected from formal standards" (Arms et al., 2002). Federation, refers to the case where the digital library sends search criteria to multiple remote repositories and the results are gathered, combined, and presented to user (Shen, 2006). In 1984 the Z39.50 protocol, which is a federated model, developed by the Linked Systems Project (LSP) project for libraries, publishers and information service providers, can be considered as a US National

Standard. This protocol has been long used in libraries for searching and retrieving bibliographic information and is supported by the US Library of Congress (Needlman, 2000).

Two systems, client and server, are used in this model. The server undertakes to update and respond to queries. The client undertakes to connect with end-users, receive queries from end-users, and send, receive and mix received responses from the server, finally presenting them to end-user. In fact, relations between client and server can be established by certain protocols. There is need to standardize query language and data storage following the same standard in all systems. The other way of running this model can be installed by middleware. The middleware undertakes contact with servers and the user just can make access to resources in other collections along with this middleware and do not need to have any relation with server.

Personalized retrieval and summarization of image, video, and language resources (PERSIVAL) is a project in Colombia University that work in the federated model. In fact, Green et al. (2001) described how they combined simple digital library interoperability protocol (SDLIP) and STAnford protocol proposal for Internet ReTrieval and Search (STARTS), two complementary protocols, for searching over distributed document collections. The resulting protocol, which they called SDARTS, is simple yet expressible enough to enable building sophisticated Meta search engines.

Support for Z39.50, a protocol that works in the federated model, in Greenstone is provided through YAZ, open source software, library that can be used by both Z39.50 clients and servers. In fact, Z39.50 serving capabilities are added to Greenstone by developing a new server that uses YAZ as a front end to accept requests from Z39.50 clients and translate them into requests that use the Greenstone protocol. The Greenstone response is then converted, through YAZ, into Z39.50 terms and returned to the client (Witten and Bainbridge, 2003).

Another project that works in the federated model is the Colorado digitization program which was established in 1998 through a library services and technology act grant through the Colorado state library. This project also uses Z39.50, like Greenstone, in order to be interoperable. DC builder is an applicant that uses in the project in order to convert metadata from a variety of systems and formats to Dublin Core (DC) as a metadata standard which is used in the systems. In a PhD thesis by Shi (2005) entitled "Lightweight federation of non-cooperating digital libraries", the researcher studied federated and harvesting models and finally proposed the federated model because of not having up to date central metadata records.

ZMARKO is used in another project in order to gather bibliographic records from 12 state libraries in Illinois, USA. ZMARKO acts as a data provider allowing MARC records available through a Z39.50 server to be made available via the OAI-PMH (Kazmarek and Naun, 2005). In fact, project team member, Tom Habing, developed an OAI-PMH/Z39.50 gateway for the purpose of creating an appropriate response to OAI-PMH requests layered over the Z39.50 server. The system works partly in a federated model by using Z39.50.

2. Harvesting model : "The difficulty of creating large federations is the motivation behind recent efforts to create looser groupings of digital libraries. The underlying concept is that the participants agree to take small efforts that enable some basic shared services, without being required to adopt a complete set of agreements" (Arms et al., 2002). Furthermore, "The Open Archives Initiative (OAI) is based around the concept of metadata harvesting. In this model, each digital library makes metadata about its collections available in a simple exchange format. This metadata can be harvested by service providers and built into services such as information discovery or reference linking" (Arms et al., 2002).

Metadata harvesting was first developed by the harvest project in the early 1990s, but the approach was not widely adopted (Bowman et al., 1994). The concept was revived in 1998 in a prototype known as the universal preprint server (Van De Sompel et al., 2000). This prototype concluded in favor of metadata harvesting as a strategy to facilitate the creation of federated services across heterogeneous preprint systems. The OAI, which is derived from this experiment, emphasizes the core functionality that can be achieved by digital libraries sharing metadata. It minimizes the cost by using a simple protocol based on HTTP, by providing software that is easily added to web servers, and by documentation, training and support (Lagoze and Van de Sompel, 2001).

In the harvesting model, DLs – which are members of a consortium, agree to interoperate with each other. Hence, they establish a server in order to present services so each library could update their data on the server by means of a simple protocol such as HTTP. Users refer to the server to retrieve information. Having regard to an agreed standard in storage and sharing metadata and also using open achieves for making access facility to information by server are the primary necessities of using this model. In this way, server undertakes to present services related to the DL's integrated data. Therefore, the possibility of integrated searching in many of DLs is procured for users.

Another way of installing this model is depicted. The difference of this way according to the previous one is in DLs two-way relation with a server. In this case, each one of the members has a copy of the integrated data in server – thus, each of the libraries is a support system for the others and mirror them. Another way of installing this model could be presented by eliminating the server in a complicated way. In this case, two-way relationships would be made possible between DLs.

Maamar (1998) in his PhD thesis in University´ Laval (Canada) expressed how an interoperable environment can be built, using teams of software agents integrated in software agent-oriented framework architecture. He and his colleagues propose the Conception par Frameworks Orientes-Agents Logiciels (C-FOAL) – Concept of software agent-oriented framework method for the development of interoperable environments. The C-FOAL method is applied to the System information Geographies et Agent Logiciel (SIGAL) project, which aims at developing an interoperable environment for geo-referenced digital libraries. To design and develop the interoperability environment SIGAL, they chose three types of frameworks (Server, Client and Logical source) in order to create a multi-framework architecture. This architecture is based on the Client/Server approach, the mirror sites, and the dynamic generation of client frameworks.

Suleman (2002) in his PhD thesis entitled Open Digital Libraries, proposed the Harvesting model with OAI protocol. Also, networked digital library of theses and dissertations (NDLTD) is a project with 13 members all over the world. As Suleman and Fox (2003) in their research article mentioned, the OAI protocol is used in this project. Also, electronic theses and dissertation metadata set (ETDMS) is used in this project as metadata standard. Harvesting model with OAI protocol is also used in National Science Digital Library (NSDL) so as to metadata harvesting in central repository (Arms et al., 2003; Lagoze et al., 2006).

OAISter in the University of Michigan uses OAI protocol for metadata harvesting, DC metadata standard with XML format. The team members expected to harvest DC encoded metadata in XML format from OAI-enabled metadata repositories, use XSLT to transform that DC metadata into DLXS bibliographic class encoded metadata, the project's native format, index the metadata and make it available to end-users through an interface that used the XPAT search engine (Hagedorn, 2003).

NASA is also using the harvesting model with the OAI protocol to make accessible their scientific and technical information in ten NASA centers and headquarters and over 50 foreign countries in order to maintain access to the largest collections of aerospace science and technical information in the world. DC is factually metadata standard for bibliographic information and PDF format for full-text information that was used in the project (Nelson et al., 2003). Also, Greenstone, open source software, is capable to be interoperable with others in Federated, Harvesting and Gathering models, through Exchange center application (Bainbridge et al., 2006).

Moreover, China Networked Digital Library of Theses and Dissertations (CNDLTD) is a project that first appeared in 1996, as a means of coordinating electronic theses and dissertations (ETD) efforts among Chinese Universities. The CNDLTD project has been carried out by China Academic Library and Information System (CALIS) and the model applied is the harvesting model with OAI protocol. DC is a metadata standard and PDF is a repository format for full-text data that are used in this project. Each member is responsible for updating their data in a central metadata list (Jin, 2004). In order to harvest bibliographic data from 12 state libraries in Illinois, USA, Kazmarek and Naun (2005) in their research article, mentioned that they used the harvesting model by OAI-PMH besides the federated model by Z39.50.

In January 2002, the National Science Council (NSC) of Taiwan launched a National Digital Archives Program (NDAP) in which many universities and research organizations participated. The project utilizes the OAI-PMH to harvest bibliographic records and DC as metadata standard and XML format as structured language (Yu et al., 2005). Interoperability between Utah universities in the USA is another project that used the harvesting model with OAI protocol and DC for metadata standard. They also, as noted previously, add ZContent applications in order to support the federated model (Arlitsch and Jonsson, 2005).

Interoperability between CDS/ISIS systems is another project, which is proposed by Jayakanth et al. (2006), for using the harvesting model. In the project CDSOAI is used as middleware between data providers and service providers to establish interoperability between systems. As well as ARC, open source software, is used to integrate data providers. Libraries in the University of Arizona system in order to exchange their digital journals started their interoperability project from April 2005. They used resource description framework (RDF) as repository standard, Qualified DC as metadata standard, and OAI-PMH as interoperability protocol (Han, 2006).

Bell and Lewis (2006), in their research article entitled using OAI-PMH and METS for exporting metadata and digital objects between repositories, studied DSpace, Fedora, and UKETD applications in the case of interoperability. DSpace is used in University of Wales Aberystewyth (UWA), Fedora is used in National Library of Wales (NLW), and UKETD is used in Electronic Theses Online Service (ETHOS). The proposed model in the article in order to exchange electronic theses between three repositories is harvesting model with OAI-PMH.. The researcher proposed a world schema for metadata repository and harvesting the resources in a central database.

In fact, D-Space, open source software, is used in this project for storage and retrieval of information. The HKUST is accessible for all users all over the world using OAI-PMH. In fact, OAISter and Scirus can simply retrieve the HKUST metadata via the OAI protocol. Qualified DC is used for metadata repository, and PDF is used for full-text data in the HKUST (Lam and Chan, 2007). Finally,

Alipour-Hafezi (2008) studied interoperability between Iranian web-based library software. He proposed a model based on the harvesting model with OAI according to their current situation. His suggestion for metadata repository standard was DC.

Generally speaking 17 projects briefly described in this section are using the harvesting model via OAI protocol and nearly all of them are using DC as metadata standard. As mentioned in the previous section, three of them are simultaneously working with harvesting and federated models.

3. Gathering model : According to Arms et al. (2002) "Even if formal cooperation between various organizations is not achievable, a base model of interoperability is still possible by gathering openly accessible information using a web search engines. Because there is no cost to the collections, gathering can provide services that embrace large numbers of digital libraries, but the services are of poorer quality than can be achieved by partners who cooperate directly" (Arms et al., 2002). They go on to say that "Some the most interesting web research at present can be thought of as adding extra function to the base level, which will lead to better interoperability, even among totally non-cooperating organizations. Even though the concept of a fully semantic web is a pipe dream, it is reasonable to expect that the level of services that can be provided by gathering will improve steadily. Research Index (formerly known as CiteSeer) is a superb example of a digital library built automatically by gathering public accessible information" (Arms et al., 2002). In fact, this model, because of being more public, was only introduced, and except for the Research Index and Exchange center software that was described in the previous section, there is no other DL project to be discussed here.

Research Issues and Priorities The working groups outlined a wide range of important research issues; most groups were less successful at prioritizing them, beyond the immediate infrastructure needs already discussed. The five key research areas that emerged from the workshop are described below; arguably, the first three are of most central and immediate importance, specifically to the development of digital libraries, though the long-term importance of research in the fifth area (economic, social, and legal issues) cannot be overemphasized. The distinctions among the five areas are to some extent arbitrary; for example, progress on interoperability (the first area) depends critically on progress in our ability to describe successfully objects and repositories (the second area).

1. Interoperability : The difficulty in defining the objectives for interoperability have already been discussed; clarifying these objectives, mapping the spectrum of interoperability, and establishing the key challenges at points along this specturm are key research issues in their own right. The more technical interoperability research involve protocol design that supports a broad range of interaction types, inter-repository protocols, distributed search protocols and technologies (including the ability to search across heterogeneous databases with some level of semantic consistency), and object interchange protocols. Interoperability is not simply a matter of providing coherence among passive object repositories. Digital library systems offer a range of services, and these services must be projected in an interoperable fashion as well. One particular issue that emerged was that existing Internet protocols (such as HTTP, the basis of the World Wide Web) are clearly inadequate. Research must move beyond the current base of deployed protocols and systems. This raises complex questions about how to deploy prototype systems and the trade-offs between advanced capabilities and ubiquity of access. The practical question of the nature of the installed technology base and the need to support this installed base will increasingly frame and influence interoperability research.

Access to digital libraries is not an end in itself for most users, but rather a support service; many will be willing to sacrifice advanced functionality for consistency, stability, and ability to use familiar, common access tools. Just as the installed base has become the greatest barrier to meaningful large-scale trials of new approaches that improve existing services (as opposed to providing entirely new services which do not compete with an installed base) in the overall Internet environment, user expectations and the installed base will ultimately impede progress in fundamental technology research within the large-scale experiments necessary to gain insights into interoperability among digital libraries. Managing this tension will be a critical element in the continued development of the community's research agenda. It should be noted that, at this relatively early stage in the evolution of digital library technology, it is of vital importance that projects strive for approaches that incorporate high functionality and extensibility. A high level of functionality in the standards and protocols used, even if not fully exploited initially, will postpone the time when the inertia of the installed base begins to confine research opportunities. Careful design of extensibility in digital library systems will facilitate continued research progress and understanding of the impact of new approaches on the user community without the need to attempt to displace an installed base.

2. Description of Objects and Repositories : In order to provide a coherent view of collections of digital objects, they must be described in a consistent fashion which can facilitate the use of mechanisms such as protocols that support distributed search and retrieval from disparate sources. Research in description of objects and collections of objects provides the foundation for effective interoperability. Interoperability at the level of deep semantics will require breakthroughs in description as well as retrieval, object interchange, and object retrieval protocols. Issues here include the definition and use of metadata and its capture or computation from objects, the use of computed descriptions of objects, federation and integration of heterogeneous repositories with disparate semantics, clustering and automatic hierarchical organization of information, and algorithms for automatic rating, ranking, and evaluation of information quality, genre, and other properties. Other key issues involved knowledge representation and interchange, and the definition and interchange of ontologies for information context. The idea of active "information matchmaking" emerged in several group reports. Research is also needed to understand the strengths and limitations of purely computer-based technologies for describing objects and repositories, and the appropriate roles for the efforts of human librarians and subject experts in the digital library context as a complement to these technology-based approaches.

3. Collection Management and Organization : Collection management and organization research is the area where traditional library missions and practices are reinterpreted for the digital library environment. Progress in this area is essential if digital library collections are to meet successfully the needs of their user communities. Policies and methods for incorporating information resources on the network into managed collections, rights management, payment, and control issues were all identified as central problems in the management of digital collections. Approaches to replication and caching of information and their relationship to collection management in a distributed environment need careful examination. The authority and quality of content in digital libraries is of central concern to the user community; ensuring and identifying these attributes of content calls for research that spans both technical and organizational issues. Research is also needed to clarify the roles of librarians and institutions in defining and managing collections in the networked environment. With the enhanced potential to support nontextual content effectively in the digital library environment, issues in nontextual and multimedia information capture, organization, and storage, indexing and retrieval are clearly key research areas. However, textual digital documents remain a vitally important research area in their own right, and are far from fully understood. The role of knowledge bases in digital libraries remains a poorly explored but potentially important question. The preservation of digital content for long periods of time, across multiple generations of hardware and software technologies and standards is essential in the creation of effective digital libraries. This is an extraordinarily difficult research problem which has not received sufficient attention.

4. User Interfaces and Human-Computer Interaction : While user interfaces and human-computer interaction issues are an extensive field of research in their own right, there are some specific problems that are central to progress in digital libraries. Display of information, visualization and navigation of large information collections, and linkages to information manipulation/analysis tools were identified as key areas for research. The use of more sophisticated models of user behavior and needs in long-term interactions with digital library systems is a potentially fruitful area for research. The necessity for a more comprehensive understanding of user needs, objectives, and behavior in employing digital library systems was stressed repeatedly as a basis for designing effective systems. Finally, it was observed that digital library systems must become far more effective in adapting to variations in the capabilities of user workstations and network connections (bandwidth) in presenting appropriate user interfaces; new technologies such as personal digital assistants and nomadic computing models will emphasize this need.

5. Economic, Social, and Legal Issues : Digital libraries are not simply technological constructs; they exist within a rich legal, social, and economic context, and will succeed only to the extent that they meet these broader needs. Rights management, economic models for the use of electronic information, and billing systems to support these economic models will be needed. User privacy needs to be carefully considered. There are complex policy issues related to collection development and management, and preservation and archiving. Existing library practice may shed some light on these questions. The social context of digital documents, including authorship, ownership, the act of publication, versions, authenticity, and integrity require a better understanding. Research in all of these areas will also be needed if digital libraries are to be successful.

USER INTERFACES

A digital library may provide a single point of access to a huge quantity of multimedia information that is available to a variety of kind users with a different psychological, educational, social backgrounds and information needs over Internet. Huge sum of money have been spent on building useable digital libraries. However research has shown that digital libraries are under utilized.

Digital libraries are inherently interactive systems with a constant growth of the number of end-users. They must not only rely on effective and sophisticated retrieval mechanisms but also provide efficient interaction with the end users.

From last two decades, several information scientists have paid attention to Human Computer Interaction (HCI) and the user interface design for information retrieval systems as well as a digital libraries. In order to enhance the usability and the accessibility of digital libraries, it is needed to show how theories and models from the domain of HCI can be applied to the user interface design of digital libraries.

User Interface Design Principles for Digital Libraries Designing an interface for digital libraries is a complex process that is oriented towards demonstration of the system's potential capabilities. Careful consideration of both system and user characteristics is the key to success for effective design. A design is considered universally usable when it addresses typical features relating to users, such as computer literacy, physical disability, competence in a foreign language, age group, or proficiency in the field of digital library content. By considering the different user requirements and technical feasibilities, we propose the following user interface design principles for digital libraries for an effective user interaction and implementation.

1. Simple : Uni-dimensional judgments span (the span of immediate memory) is usually somewhere in the neighbourhood of seven, ± two. This essentially means that humans have a very small (5-9 chunks of unrelated information) short-term memory load. So, the DL User Interface should be simple and straightforward. Basic functions should be immediately apparent, while advanced functions may be less obvious to new users. A well-organized interface that supports user tasks fades into the background and allows users to work efficiently. Functions like Copy, Print, and Save etc should be included only if a task analysis shows need/necessity for them. The best interface is one that is not noticed, and one that permits the user to focus on the information and task at hand instead of the mechanisms used to present the information and perform the task.

2. Support : The DL User Interface should provide users to control over the DL; it has to enable the users to accomplish tasks using any sequence of steps that they would naturally use. UI should not limit them by artificially restricting their choices to system notion of the "correct" sequence. It should be more on event driven rather than menu driven. The user interface of a system should support for different tasks. Most users perform a variety of tasks and may be expert at some and novices at others. Besides providing assistance when requested, the system should recognize and anticipate the user's goals and offer assistance to make the task easier. Ideally, assistance should improve user's knowledge that will allow them to accomplish their tasks quickly. Intelligent assistance is like the training wheels on a bicycle - at some point, most users will want to take them off and go forward on their own. The assistance should allow them to become independent at some point when they choose to be so.

3. Familiar : The UI of DL should be familiar to its users by allowing them to build on prior knowledge, especially knowledge they have gained from experience in the real world. Users should not have to learn new things to perform familiar tasks. The use of concepts and techniques that users already understand from their real world experiences allows them to get started quickly and make progress immediately.

4. Informative Feedback : The UI of DL must provide informative feedbacks to its user. As a general rule, there must be user feedback for every user action. As to the extent and form of feedback, it is dependent on the task that is performed. For minor and frequent actions, the feedback could be subtle, for instance a change of the content of the page or a soft sound will suffice. For major actions, for instance the changing of passwords or error messages, the feedback should be more obvious in the form of pop-ups and/ or jarring noises to alert the user of the situation.

5. Design Dialogues to Yield Closure : Informative feedback at the completion of a series of actions will give operators a satisfaction of accomplishment and to prepare for the next group of actions.

6. Prevent Errors : The system should be designed in such a way that user cannot make serious errors. Any avenue of making errors should be minimized. Another way is to make the system insensitive to errors. The UI of DL should provide a mechanism to detect the user errors and offer simple, constructive and speciûc instructions that users can understand.

7. Multimedia Support : Today's information is not only the textual information but also a variety kind of data such as maps, photographs, audio and video etc. Digital Libraries are providing this kind of rich multimedia information. So, the UI of DL must support the multimedia information.

8. Proûle Based Support : Digital Libraries are maintaining the user proûles in order to provide efûcient services. The UI of DL must act according to the settings speciûed in the user's proûle and the settings should be changeable from time to time by the users.

9. Lithe and Simple : Most of the DLs are accessible to users through Internet only. Possibly normal/home user's connectivity of Internet is less in speed and research has shown that for most of the computing tasks, the threshold of frustration is about ten seconds. Hence the user interface of the digital library must be lithe and simple without having heavy and unnecessary graphics which causes burden on network trafûc and unnecessary delay.

10. Pan and Zoom Support : User interactions are based on the familiar ideas of pan and zoom. A user can zoom out and see the whole collection but with little detail, zoom in part way to see sections of the collection, or zoom in to see every detail. This spatial approach makes extensive use of research in human perception. Since people have good spatial memory, the system emphasizes shape and position as clues to help people explore information and to recall later what they found. So, the UI of DL has to support the Pan and Zoom features, and this should also be proûle based.

11. Accuracy : Poor display of information, spelling

errors and grammatical errors display poor maintenance and it affects the site's credibility. So, UI of DL should provide accurate information as much as possible to the user in a proper display mode.

12. Efficient Searching with NLP support : Most of the users visit digital libraries for getting the required information on searching and browsing it. Digital Library has to provide the efûcient search mechanisms with excellent search interface support. In order to search the DL most of the user quires are in natural language only. The emergence and ever increasing importance of end user searching provides challenging opportunities for the integration of sophisticated natural language analysis and processing techniques in user-friendly interfaces. Natural language interface technology represents a major break-through in "user friendly" computer systems.

13. Support of Semantic approach and Resource Description Frame Work (RDF) Technologies : Semantic approach and RDF technologies are providing easy and efûcient way of searching to the user. By enabling these technologies in designing of UI of DL will give more beneûts to users in their interactions with the DL.

14. Sharing and Reusing of Information : The interface needs to support sharing and reusing the information processing knowledge. In a computerized environment, the searches of users can be easily recorded and re-used. The following are the mechanisms for using this information to improve future searching efûciency.

- Collaborative ûltering.
- Social ûltering/recommending.

15. Multilingual Support : At present most of the digital libraries are portals. The availability of knowledge and information is not only in one language; hence the user interface of digital library must support the multilingual support.

16. Platform Independent : Since the digital libraries are running on Internet, the user's environment may not be the same; hence the user interface of digital library must be platform independent and adoptable to all types of environments.

17. Future Plug-ins Support : Development in technologies and ever increasing human needs are providing new types of information access. To support future information needs the UI of DL must be capable and adoptable for future developments.

CONCLUSION

There is no doubt that the utility of digital libraries as they facilitate live and interactive access to wide variety of content online. But the problems of managing digital library content and its development are manifold. Management of digital library content requires two prolonged strategies: i) to digitize local content; and ii) to devise options for accessing external resources. Generally there is a feeling that publishers copyright most of the contents available in our library, and we are not in a position to provide online access to those contents. Though our libraries are facing a shortage of content, there is a wide spectrum of formal and informal sources available with them but could be converted into digital form by devising suitable action plan. Image format, compression schemes, network transmission, monitor and printer design, computing capacity, and image-processing capabilities are all likely to improve dramatically over the next decade. But technology alone will not determine the future; relationship, economic and pattern of behavior are equally important.

Digitization is the first step in building digital libraries. Besides digitization of documents achieves the purpose of preservation for the future generations and also supports the traditional library mission of collection development, organization, and access to presentation.

Digital documents facilitate search and retrieval and can easily accessible worldwide once they are made available on the Internet.

The main object of interoperability in DLs is to build their full-text data accessible for their users. In other words, users in DLs want to get access to information resources which placed in DL which are a member of it or other DLs. Thus, DLs should pay attention to make consortiums with other ones so as to make their information resources accessible for users. DLs should also prepare facilities to exchange full-text data between each other and also other information centers.

QUESTIONS

1. Define user interfaces of digital library ?
2. Describe digital library management ?
3. Define Design of digital library?
4. Define Interoperability of digital libraries?

3
Digital Content Creation

INTRODUCTION

The advent of digital libraries at the turn of the twenty-first century has been mired with several aspects including the development of appropriate technologies, issues related to storage, rights management, and so on. Digital libraries, along with associated technologies and related issues, are still somewhat in infancy with very few fully established digital libraries the world over. The concept of digital libraries itself varies greatly with several known definitions. With digital library technologies maturing, storage capacities increasing and digital access improving, the focus needs to be crystallized on content for digital libraries. However, research on digital libraries so far has focused on the containers and conduits rather than the contents. A recent review of digital libraries in India found that out of 63 studies, only two have discussed about content in comparatively greater details (Mahesh and Mittal, 2008). Other studies also reflect a similar trend (Bearman, 2007; Fox and Urs, 2002). This clearly shows that digital library creators as of today focus less on content compared to other aspects. Consequently, it may be appropriate to conclude that copyright issues with regard to content in digital libraries are hardly on the radar of digital library creators.

Although, digital library creators presently focus on areas other than content, the creators realize that content is the key for success. It has been reported that for the success of information gateways, the effective selection of high-quality content forms the chief rationale for the gateway approach. The content includes selection criteria, technical and policy issues, management, recommended standards and conventions, creation of metadata, provision of browsing and searching (Heery, 2000).

Digital content creation requires strategic leadership, sustainability plans, and cognizance of best practice in the field. During creation of digital content, staff gain valuable skills that can be utilized by taking contract projects. This will also create new audiences for such types of material there by opening up the collections to the world. However, high-quality digital content creation is an expansive undertaking (McMenemy, 2007).

It is well known that in a largely print based traditional library setting, acquiring the content is a relatively easy task. But this is not the case with digital libraries. The variability of digital content per se and the variability in the availability of content is increasingly becoming a problem for digital libraries. Variability of digital content per se include the types of content such as text, audio, video, pictures, etc. types of file formats such as DOC, PDF, JPEG, AVI, and so on. Variability with regard to availability of digital content include the origin and sourcing of the content, creation of content, etc. which is discussed in greater detail in this paper. Normalizing, these and other varied content in digital libraries may be less challenging today owing to technological developments. But choosing content in light of copyright issues may be a daunting task. Although, the copyright issues with regard to digital content have been a subject of discussion in earlier studies, the same have not been looked at from the content creation point of view.

Objectives

The objectives of this module are to discuss and impart knowledge on the following aspects of digital library

- Introduce the concept of digital content creation;
- Discusses digital library initiatives in India.
- To evaluate the problem of digital initiatives in digital library.

CONTENT CREATION

Content creation is needed to showcase your things in a systematic way to your users. In traditional library process also library professionals use do this work in a daily basis to satisfy their users but it is not documented. Documenting this daily processes and making it to be used by wide range of users is the main idea behind content creation. The development of newsworthy, educational and entertainment material for distribution over the Internet or other electronic media.

Content creation is the contribution of information to any media and most especially to digital media for an end-user / audience in specific contexts.

Content is "something that is to be expressed through some medium, as speech, writing or any of various arts" for self -expression, distribution, marketing and/or publication.

For ex: Suppose a researcher comes in an academic library asking help for a list of document available on his topic of research. Then the list is made with the help of the catalogue and with the skill of the professional and may be provided to the cliental, but this list is not kept for further use. If the same list is stored for further use or in the age of IT is uploaded in the website for the wide range of users this is treated as content creation. Like this many of the reference services are being provided daily by the professional likewise they:

- Produce a pathfinder or a tip-sheet hand out;
- Write a book review;
- Create a newsletter or blog specifically for patrons;
- Author original stories for story time; or
- Develop and led programs and classes

The same can be uploaded in a place and is provided to wide range of users. Similarly libraries can create a lot of content with the help of latest technology and the expertise and skill and help their users. Library websites can be framed to have videos, podcasts and blog platform and these can be used as medium of communication of contents created by libraries. Similarly here are other ways by which libraries can create content for readers:

Videos : Libraries can upload videos of the specific services they provide to the users in YouTube Channel and Face book to reach large range of users.

Podcasts : Libraries can capture audio of programs by library hosts and send out as a podcast. They can create weekly or monthly podcast shows. It can include discussions on library resources and collections by special guests from the library and community which will help the users learn about new bestsellers and emerging genres. It will help the reader to know what others are reading and recommending. This type of practice is common in foreign countries among public libraries. Same can be done by academic libraries where teachers or lecturer can review a book and recommend the same for the students or colleagues.

Blog posts : Simple blogs from libraries about latest arrival can help an entire community and it can be updated time to time. This can also include some news about library that they like to communicate among the users.

DIGITAL LIBRARIES AND CONTENT CREATION

Digital libraries, by virtue of how content has been created and made available, can be broadly grouped into three classes: born digital, turned digital, and gained digital libraries.

Born digital

The advent of the internet has seen the voluminous growth of born digital material (Taylor, 2004). In born digital libraries, the content is created in digital form with the purpose and understanding that the content is primarily meant for storage and use in digital form. The tools for creating such born digital content can include simple word processing package or complex multimedia content authoring and development tools. In the past, i.e. in the print based traditional library era, the role of library as a publisher has been marginal. Leaving aside the bibliographies, catalogues, guides, and other masses of printed ephemera that such libraries have been producing, the concept of publishing a booklet or book with the library's imprint have not been common (Field, 1979). However, in the present digital age it has become possible for libraries to play a more indulgent role as publisher. The content creation job itself being left to the students, researchers or faculty of the institution concerned. The libraries are usually entrusted with the responsibility of publishing or hosting the content on the digital library or digital repository of the institution.

Wherever, the library wants to be directly involved in content creation, the libraries can do so themselves or commission or collaborate with content creators to develop user specific contents. And depending on the agreed upon modalities for content creation, the digital libraries can ensure that the copyright rests with the digital library.

Born digital content can be categorized into exclusive digital wherein the analog version is not developed at all. This could include creating curriculum focused content, e-books, learning objects or other multimedia content where analog counterparts are not meant to be created or are not required. The other type of born digital content type is digital for print. In this type, the content is created in digital form for dual purposes, which include hosting the content in digital libraries and also having a print counterpart of the content so developed. Many books and journals publishers follow this model of content creation.

The problem with born digital content is that content creation can be a time consuming task taking a long time to populate the digital library. Further, resource requirement in terms of manpower and financial resources would be high for the content creation process. Recently, with institutional repositories and archives gaining popularity and in some instances being mandatory, the content creation keeps the digital requirements in perspective although a print counterpart such as a journal or a thesis is also produced.

Turned digital

In the turned digital type, the contents that are in analog form such as the printed books are converted to digital form. Digitization technologies particularly the scanning technology is exploited to turn analog material existing on print media including paper, manuscripts, etc. to digital form and storing them in digital form only. Digitization technologies are also improving day by day making it easier to turn analog content into digital content. Major digital library initiatives in the world such as Project Gutenberg and the Million Book Project belong to the turned digital library kind.

Based on the type of conversion involved, the turned digital kind can be categorized as turned digital with replica content and turned digital with modified content. In the former kind, the digital content is an exact replica of the print counter part. Cover to cover scanning and digitized books, theses, etc. are exact digital copies of the print counterpart. But for some materials, this kind of scanning is not suitable such as for an abstracting publication. Such material is turned digital by keying in the entire content or doing an optical character recognition (OCR) scanning where editable text results from the scanning process. However, the accuracy levels of OCR scanning are low and require editing of the converted text. Turned digital content, the scanned image or the OCR text are the most common types of content in digital libraries particularly for dated content that exist in print form only and require to be converted to digital form.

The disadvantages of turned digital content include the large size of the resultant scanned file which can become time consuming to download for voluminous publications. With regard to copyright issues, digitizing "out of copyright" material and institution owned copyrighted material such as dissertation and thesis is easier but obtaining permissions from copyright owners of other desired materials is a daunting task.

Gained digital

In the gained digital type, the content per se might have been born digital or turned digital at some source but the library is not associated with the creation of content. The library only acts as a facilitator to access the already available content. This could include licensed resources such as the e-journals, e-books, databases, etc. to which through licensing mechanisms, the library facilitates access to these resources but do not own the content themselves. The content is hosted by the licensors such as the publishers themselves and the libraries facilitate access to the content without the library actually owning the content. In another form, the library could have acquired or purchased the digital content on media such as CD-ROM and DVD-ROM and have hosted it on the library computing infrastructure. Though very high costs are involved in developing a gained digital content in the library collection, the consortium access ensures that high-quality resources can be made available to the users in the shortest time and content is easier to manage. However, considering that content is usually licensed, the perpetuality of the digital content can be a problem area. Furthermore, the users should be sensitized about the copyright issues involved as the library is likely to have entered into licensing agreements with publishers or other intermediaries with regard to the usage of the content.

MANAGEMENT OF DIGITAL LIBRARIES

The steps including: various representative sample of candidates involved in all higher educational institutions as view above, learning process and active teaching methods implied for the teaching and blended in the context of the materials, formulated approaches to collaborations (Fredrick Kiwuwa Lugya, 2018) website and partnerships, visited different types of libraries to benchmark library practices and encourage job opportunity, understand and respect to all other's work to change their activities with mindsets. College librarians are advised to handle priorities of the library that on the rules by activities of the place indicates by agenda. Our short-term activities are UFL training gives practical layout and training with the individual, group tasks, discussions, assignments and finally by the presentation. This improved to participate and develop the study material and active responsibility of work done by them.

Throughout the world, most libraries offer informational RDM services like assistance. It is the separate branch of traditional reference consultation in using, locating, and citing data and datasets. Along with the existing skill sets of experienced personnel are doing the large part. Data Management Plan on the consultation on particular focus areas likely changes the Research Data Management technical (Bethany Latham, 2017) services of the libraries. The RMD services covered with involvement, creating and needs various supports from the technical repository and updated systems, and also providing placement with those technical repositories. These services are never removed ion technical know-how and large dominated data are already collected in data curation, still many libraries are not with the single-handle repositories they are having datasets on various organizational structure.

Librarians must be aware of services by campus or outstation or through the online and professional conference to learn the opportunity (Carol Tenopir, 2014) of services for the research students for the continuing education and also know the knowledge apart from the subjects. Still, they are not using Digital Libraries (DL), this is the major challenge by the assist like text mining, Bibliometric (Philipp Mayr and Ingo Frommholz, 2018) data retrieval and needed in language processing techniques was adopted.

Libraries are predictable to prove their value stand to from their users. Smart and marketing service (Ilka Datig, 2018) an effective manner, resources, and space of supporters are the portion of demonstrating value. Libraries involved with marketing are highly idea taken from profit business organization in the world. All businesses are a risk in the same way publisher's fear is high, which involved publishing houses and make business (Martin Zimerman, 2011) in profit motto. The thoughts of a businessman, when they realized that profits are subverted, which leads to a panic situation.

The end result of the study shows that performance and effort expectancy, social influence, conditions of facilitating and behavioral intention (Muhammad Arif, 2018) of students are measured majority are from the web service user. Among the factors, the student behavioral intention was found to be the strongest predictor in measuring the actual use. The moderating effect in age, gender and experience did not have any impact on the factors.

CHALLENGES IN MANAGEMENT OF DIGITAL LIBRARIES

The study indicates the primary goal of the local researcher's concerns and challenges in Data Management Methods. There is a lack of perceived time space and opportunity to the campus in discussions and develop plans for students, faculty and the supporting units. Some argue that research conducted at master's level institutions and not the knowledge to the general body. Interest cum involvement is the most important aspect to the research faculty who are in the study, for intellectual growth in personal, to improve the teaching style in program and career advancement.

There is a change in workflows of the professional librarians on ERM (Michael Breaks, 1999) basic work by the paraprofessionals, still, questions regarding on professionals and paraprofessional who are responsible for a particular task in ERM work. This causes uncertainty of workflows, in the same way it gives additional time to focus on activities like negotiating their licenses and ERM task related works. The question which is raised to know the library activities (Carol Tenopir, 2014) whether they actively engage their service, future manpower requirement, education background and having a self-learning opportunity. On these solutions are needed for librarians to learn more from the professionals, by attending workshops and also in their own campus.

The report of this group, as invest to save (Seamus Ross and Margaret Hedstrom, 2005) the research challenges need to make progress development of digital library era. The investment in library needed comes from public sources, and voluntary industries making substantial technology and services. E-Resources provide the mechanism to build up the purchase (Terri Muraski, 2016) databases and E-Books packages. In addition to that a set of electronic reference resources mainly subscribed by many libraries, providing high-quality information in the library and outside the library that is workplace or home. If any mislead and problem arise the guidance of these resources and in terminology usage across various library services (David McMenemy, 2012) is inconsistency.

There is a reason behind, some people will never speak with the librarian, these supporters represent know only library context. Negative content gives a bad trust, and lose of opportunities to the patrons. Content strategy (Ilka Datig, 2018) is the way to improve revitalize and content. Now a day's academic library will face problems like E-Books. It is a beginning problem; the main problem is a multitude of copyright issues. It is the time to jump into the EBooks bandwagon. In this case, E-book readers, if the content download by their patrons will take as illegal or misused. Some scholar, researchers and students are borrowing the E-books but they are not purposefully using the resources they need.

Selection (Michael Breaks, 1999) and identifying there availability and needs, analyzing costs, choosing among formats, licenses and legal activities, interpreting service, facilities and preparing equipment, development of local approaches, cataloging and E-Resources are the new challenges. A network with high-speed data cache (William Johnston, 1997) plays a vital role in this approach, storage for incoming data, intermediate processes and as an application cache.

FILE FORMATS

The management of file formats should be considered in the wider strategic context of preservation planning. What can your organisation afford to do? How much developer effort will it require? What do the users require from your collections? Are you committing yourself to a storage problem? At all times, the answer to digital preservation issues is not to try and "do everything". Your strategy ought to move you towards simple and practical actions, rather than trying to support more file formats than you need.

The purpose of this section is not to provide a detailed or exhaustive list of current formats for different types of content but to draw attention to the broader implications of file formats for their application, and implications for preservation.

A substantial part of this chapter refers to the possible selection of a file format for migration purposes. While migration is a valid preservation strategy, and quite common for many file formats, it is not the only approach or solution. Where appropriate, the chapter will refer to other suitable methods for preservation.

In the process of digital preservation, file formats play very important role. These are the standards which incorporate the quality issues relating to information storage, file size, type of data compression and also information retrieval. Since we are moving towards 'Paperless society', the functions and strategies for achieving the basic objectives have been changed in modern Library and Information Centre. The same principal applies to the managers of archive drawings and photographic records, who have the facilities for the storage of their archives in digital format. The conversion of the original hard copy records into digital records is known as digitization. In the process of digital preservation, it is primarily essential to examine basic issues to achieve the required end product. For line drawings the question needs to be asked as to whether the drawing is likely to be used and modified or is retained as an archive. If it belongs to an archival collection, the drawing is scanned and stored as a digital file on CD-ROM or DVD. If the drawing is to be used as a working drawing on a Computer Aided Design (CAD) system, then the scanned data needs to be converted into vector data in an intelligent form i.e. in a way that replicates the same drawing if it had been produced originally on CAD.

Photographs are also scanned using the original negatives or transparencies if possible, if not then photographic prints. Old and damaged photographs can be cleaned and digitally repaired.

Three major issues related to storage of Digital information:

- The format of the digital data and any compression has a major effecting file size and a minor effect on quality.
- The resolution of the scanning is a balance between quality and file size.
- The storage medium can have an effect on retrieval times.

As computer storage is becoming less expensive, it supports to move towards higher standards, i.e. higher resolution. But it should be remembered that a relatively small increase in the resolution results in a proportionately high increase in file size.

File formats organised by content types

Different content types have, over time, developed their own file formats as they strive to accommodate functionality specific to their needs. The main content types are images, video, audio and text; however, a growing number of formats are being structured to address the demands of new media, including formats for 3D models and archiving the web.

File formats vary enormously in terms of complexity, with some data being encoded in many layers. In some cases the file formats involved are just one part of a larger picture, a picture that includes software, hardware, and even entire information environments.

File formats - what should we be worrying about?

Obsolescence

Formats evolve as users and developers identify and incorporate new functionality. New formats, or versions of formats, may introduce file format obsolescence as newer generations of software phase out support for older formats. When software does not provide for backwards compatibility with older file formats, data may become unusable. Both open source and commercial formats are vulnerable to obsolescence: vendors sometimes use planned obsolescence to entice customers to upgrade to new products while open source software communities may withdraw support for older formats if these are no longer generally needed by the community. Obsolescence can also be accidental: both businesses and open source communities can fail.

File format format obsolescence is a risk that needs to be understood. That said, the problem may not be as severe as the digital preservation community perceived it to be some 10 years ago. Many established file formats are still with us, still supported, and still usable. It is quite likely that the majority of file formats you deal with will be commonly understood and well supported.

Proliferation

Arguably, in some sectors, proliferation is more of a challenge than obsolescence. If formats aren't normalised then an organisation can end up with a large number of different file formats, and versions of those formats: e.g. lots of different versions of PDF, word, image formats etc. In domains which develop rapidly evolving bespoke data formats this problem can be exacerbated. Tracking and managing all these formats - which ones are at risk, and which tools can be used for each one - can be a serious challenge.

Your digital preservation strategy should strive to

mitigate the effects of obsolescence and proliferation. Strategies as migration, emulation, normalisation and a careful selection of file formats are all valid and worth considering, in the context of your collections and your organisation.

File Formats

a. To preserve documents, a collection's file format must ensure the following:

   i. Save the bits so that somewhere a copy survives and that copy can be found.

   ii. Ensure that the bits can be interpreted later (file format retention).

   iii. Make the bits trustworthy by reliably associating sufficient metadata.

   iv. Include library content lists among the set of saved documents.

   v. Minimize the need for digital archaeology (rescuing content from obsolete technology) through the ability to translate to other formats.

b. Which formats can preserve content or lead to a longer duration between transformations?

   i. International standards are preferred.

   ii. XML allows users to understand an object's structure and content without using specific machines or software.

   iii. Text documents (Word or other proprietary formats) depend on compatibility between software versions. XML with metadata tagging would lead to longer preservation.

   iv. PDF documents lead to PDF/A documents (archiving).

   v. Image options – TIFF, GIF, JPEG, JP2, Flashpix, ImagePac, PNG, PDF

c. Sustainability factors for file formats

   i. Adoption – used by the primary creators, disseminators, or users of information resources

   ii. Disclosure – complete specifications and tools for validating technical integrity exist and are accessible

   iii. External Dependencies – depends on particular hardware, operating system, or software

   iv. Impact of Patents – ability of archival institutions to sustain content in a format will be inhibited by patents

   v. Quality and functionality – ability of a format to represent the significant characteristics of a given content item required by current and future users

   vi. Self-documentation – contains basic descriptive, technical, and other administrative metadata

   vii. Transparency – digital representation is open to direct analysis with basic tools

   viii. Technical Protection Mechanism – implementation of mechanisms, such as encryption, that prevent the preservation of content by a trusted repository

d. File format selection is a first step in long-term preservation measures that is part of a larger information management strategy.

e. Difficult items to store or move between formats

   i. mathematical symbols

   ii. chemical formulas

   iii. archaic scripts or ideographs, such as Egyptian or Mayan hieroglyphs

   iv. musical notations

DIGITAL LIBRARY INITIATIVES

In India, a number of digital library initiatives and digitization programmes have been initiated across the country. Some of the important initiatives are discussed below.

Digital Library of India

Digital Library of India (DLI) is the biggest national level digital library initiative in India. It is a part of the Universal Digital Library Project, envisaged by Carnegie Mellon University, USA, which has some other international partners such as China and Egypt. DLI is coordinated by Indian Institute of Science, Bangalore and is supported by Ministry of Communications and Information Technology, Government of India. The Mission is to create a portal for the Digital Library of India which will foster creativity and free access to all human knowledge. As a first step in realizing this mission, it is proposed to create the Digital Library of one million books, predominantly in Indian languages, available to everyone over the Internet. This portal will also become an aggregator of all the knowledge and digital content created by other digitallibrary initiatives in India.

Traditional Knowledge Digital Library (TKDL)

A project called Traditional Knowledge Digital Library (TKDL) initiated in 2001 is a collaborative one between Council of Scientific and Industrial Research (CSIR), Ministry of Science and Technology and Department of AYUSH, Ministry of Health and Family Welfare, which is implanted at CSIR. TKDL preserves the information in languages and formats understandable by the patent examiners at International Patent Officers (IPOs), to avoid issuing of patent wrongly. Many personnel such as technical experts, team of traditional medicine, Information Technology experts, patent examiners and scientists are involved in the project. This project involves in documenting traditional knowledge such as Ayurveda, siddha, Unani, Yoga in digitized form in five international languages (English, German, French, Japanese, and Spanish)

Down the Memory Lane

The National Library of India has initiated in late 1990s a digitization programme, known as 'Down the Memory Lane', to digitize rare books, manuscripts and other resources from its collection. The English books that were published prior to 1900 and Indian books published before 1920 were taken into consideration. Similarly, the Central Secretariat Library has initiated a programme to digitize government publications like, Gazette of India, Commission & Committee Reports, Annual Reports of the Ministries.

Indira Gandhi National Centre for the Arts (IGNCA)—Kalasampada

Indira Gandhi National Centre for Arts (IGNCA), established a Digital Library, known as "Kalasampada", (Digital Library Resource for Indian Cultural Heritage). It includes non-print as well as printed mate rials. The users will have access to the highly researched publications of the IGNCA from a single window. The integration of multimedia computer technology and software provides a new dimension in the study of the Indian Art and Culture.

Indian Parliament Library

This library serves members of Parliament and officers and staff of Lok Sabha Secretariat. Large databases were initially developed by the computer centre. The data are stored and available now in PARLIS (Parliament Library Information System).

Khuda Baksh Oriental Public Library

The Khuda Baksh Oriential Public Library has initiated digitization of Arabic and Persian manuscripts of the medieval India. It is one of the Oriental Libraries having rich collection of Persian, Arabic, Urdu and other languages manuscripts.

National Mission for Manuscripts

As a part of the digitization efforts, the Department of Culture, Ministry of Tourism and Culture, Government of India, launched the National Mission for Manuscripts in February 2003.The main objectives of the mission are to facilitate conservation and preservation of manuscripts through training, awareness, and financial support; and promote access to Indian manuscripts; to encourage scholarship and research in the study of Indian languages and manuscriptology; and to build a National Manuscript Library

National Digital Library

National Digital Library is initiated by Ministry of Human Resource Development Coordinated By IIT Kharagpur. It has currently 15, 38,083 items hosted including educational materials are available for users ranging from primary to post-graduate levels. There are more than 40 types of learning resources are available, items are available in more than 70 languages. Repository integrates contents from different Indian Institutional Repositories. Repository hosts contents from multiple subject domains like Technology, Science, Humanities, Agriculture and others. MHRD sponsored project hosts 10,000+ video lectures in engineering domain; LibriVox consists of more than 2 Lakhs Audio books.

Indira Gandhi Memorial Library, University of Hyderabad

TAs well as being the first fully automated library in India, it was the first to begin a digital library program.

Since 2002 the library has digitized around 250,000 pages, primarily theses and dissertations, as well as 300 books in English and Indian languages. The library has access to about 170,000 electronic journals. The library preserves discs that accompany printed books and journals by uploading them to the CD server, which is linked to the digital library system. The library scans printed journals from Indian publishers and maintains them in the digital library as well. The library uses the open source software D-space for its institutional repository.

ETD and Institutional Repository

Theses and dissertations are the bedrock of graduate education. Thesis and dissertation research is guided by experts in the field and frequently funded by highly competitive scholarships and grants. Theses and dissertations are useful sources of secondary information, particularly in the humanities, where texts are important and ideas stay current longer. Most of these works languish in college and university libraries and archives. Electronically publishing of theses and dissertations brings this valuable material more prominence. An Institutional Repository (IR) is a digital archive of the intellectual output of a university. Theses and dissertations are one basic category of material for an IR.

Vidyanidhi Projects

Vidyanidhi (which means "treasure of knowledge" in Sanskrit) is a digital archive of dissertations, as well as a set of resources for doctoral research in India. Vidyanidhi is being developed as a national repository and a consortium for electronic dissertations, through participation and partnership with universities, academic institutions, and other stakeholders. Vidyanidhi began as a pilot project in 2000with governmental support, well as support from the Ford Foundation and Microsoft India. The Ford Foundation support is for focusing on Social and Human Sciences. The Microsoft support is for the implementation of Unicode for Indian Languages. Vidyanidhi is a member of the Networked Digital Library of Theses and Dissertations (NDLTD), and UNESCO and other efforts in this direction. UNESCO supports ETD initiatives worldwide.

Electronic Theses and Dissertation Project of INFLIBNET Centre

INLIBNET hosts a bibliographic database 200,000 dissertations from about two hundred Indian universities going back to 1905. The Repository uses D-Space, which complies with the Open Archives Initiative (OAI) framework allowing publications to be easily indexed and searched by web search engines and other indexing services.

Indian Institute of Astrophysics

The Indian Institute of Astrophysics has its origins in the Madras Observatory, which was created in the late 18 th century. Today the Institute is a national research centre for physics and astronomy. Its repository includes dissertations from researchers associated with the Institute, as well as papers from the Bulletin of the Astronomical Society India beginning with volume 1 (1973), journal articles, and conference papers. Archival materials from the 18th, 19th, and 20th centuries have recently been added. These materials are manuscripts, photographs, annual reports, instruments and their descriptions. The repository uses DSpace.

Raman Research Institute

Raman Research Institute (RRI) is located in Bangalore, Karnataka state maintains digital repository for the research community benefits. It enables the research community to submit their preprints, postprints and other publications, using single web interface is being organized and kept in repository for easy retrieval of the information. The repository is developed with D-Space open source software complies with Open Archive Initiatives (OAI) framework, which facilitates to index and search by web search engines and other indexing tools. The contents available through RRI Digital Repository are approximately 5875, which includes

- Research publication of faculty and students
- Theses
- Annual Reports
- Collected papers of C.V. Raman
- Newspaper clippings

Indian Institute of Technology, New Delhi

Digital library initiatives began in 1998 with an upgrade to a faster Internet connection. The high speed Internet connection led to a number of digitized collections. IITs receive grants from government bodies such as AICTE (All India Council of Technical Education) and the Ministry of Human Resources Development and Management (MHRD) to develop digital libraries. Online courseware has been developed and older volumes of journals have been digitized, among other projects. More than 500dissertations are available in the repository. The campus has facilities for submitting material to there pository. More than 25,000 pages of journals were scanned and are available on the Institute intranet.

Indian Institute of Science, Bangalore

The Institute uses e-Prints, an institutional repository of research output. The archive is maintained by the National Center for Science Information (NCSI) and it supports selfarchiving in various file formats (pdf, Word, html, etc.) Around 5,000 articles are available.

Indian Institute of Technology, Bombay

The repository has bibliographic information and abstract for dissertations beginning in 1965. The masters thesis database has bibliographic information and abstract from 1999 on. More than 3,000 full text theses and Dissertations are available in the ETD database. The repository uses Greenstone, open source software, which complies with the Open Archives Initiative (OAI) protocol.

National Institute of Technology, Calicut

"Nalanda" was initiated in 1999 and is one of the largest digital libraries in the country. It serves the campus with research and other academic information in science, engineering, and technology. The software used was developed by the institute itself. Nalanda is accessible from anywhere on campus. The repository contains theses and dissertations, course materials, articles, and annual reports.

National Institute of Technology, Rourkela

Formerly known as Regional Engineering College (REC), this is one of the premier institutions for technical education in the country. NIT is a joint undertaking of Government of India and Government of Orissa. This Institutional Repository uses D-Space. At present around 343 documents are available in the repository.

PROBLEMS FOR DIGITAL INITIATIVES

The digitization initiatives in India are encountered with several problems such as lack of technical infrastructure, trained manpower, finances and policy initiatives. Some of the important problems are discussed below:

- Lack of clear cut policy at National level with main focus on sustainability
- Outdated software and hardware and difficulty in upgrading the same.
- Non-availability of cost effective new technological advancement.

- Lack of multiple Indian language OCR facilities.
- Non-standard technical activities, data description and transmission characteristics.
- Non-availability of well-trained skilled personnel.
- Lack of management support
- Lack of proper preservation policy
- No Intellectual Property Rights policy for content development of digital information.
- Rigidity in the publishers' policies and data formats

OPEN ARCHIVES INITIATIVE (OAI)

The Open Archives Initiative (OAI) is a major development embedded in the digital library community to heighten interoperability and provide more targeted access to scholarly electronic full texts. The OAI has been instrumental in developing a Protocol for Metadata Harvesting (OAI-PMH) which gathers metadata from electronic full-text repositories, indexes it for searching purposes, conducts the search, and provides the metadata in a distinct format as the first step to retrieval of the full texts. To accomplish this, the metadata contained in the headers of HTML and XML documents must be compliant with the defined OAI metadata, namely unqualified Dublin Core metadata in an XML format (header information or in a database that the harvester can process). This establishes the premise that OAI metadata is standardized in its form, yet highly diverse in its content. Because the OAI-PMH allows for the use of parallel metadata sets, additional metadata can exist in the document which can be used as additional selection criteria and for more specific searching, as well as for filtering purposes. This article gives an overview of the development and philosophy of the OAI. Various implementers of the OAI are highlighted and ongoing research in the context of the total digital library research technology is described, followed by a rough sketch of the implications for the scientific community. The conclusion looks at the status of the OAI at the beginning of March 2002 and considers the time frame of the immediate future, as well as the impact of widespread adoption.

Developmental overview and context

The OAI represents the results of three major developments of the 1990s and indeed the OAI has in part gained its orientation through these developments. The research community had rapidly recognized the advantages of opening the Internet to universities and non-military research centres, as well as the vast possibilities for digital exchange of data for purposes of information provision in all areas of research and higher education.

1. The roots of the OAI lie in the efforts of scientists themselves to make the newest research results accessible by 'publishing' submitted and other published and unpublished research reports to the research community via so-called 'preprint servers'. The original motivation for creating preprint servers was to counteract publication delays and also make access available to a wider sample of the research and scientific community.
2. As a result of considerations of what digital data exchange would mean for information provision, the 'Digital Libraries Initiative' of the US National Science Foundation (1994–1998, Phase II 1998–2001) evolved, a funding programme for develop- ment of not only digital libraries but also a broad spectrum of innovative projects to increase and enhance the distribution of content and new forms of information. A primary interest was the significance of interoperability in technical, structural, and organizational dimensions which had quickly become apparent. Similarly, and ultimately necessary to achieve interoperability, the importance

of standardization of formats, the importance of metadata and data exchange and transport protocols was also quickly recognized. Hence, the first projects of the NSF programme focused on interoperability. Subsequent funding for innovation and rapid integration of technology into the information-provision structures followed in other countries.

3. Researchers and authors of journal articles had become increasingly dissatisfied with the time lag between submission of an article and its publication in a scholarly journal. At the same time skyrocketing prices for electronic journals and unjustifiably restrictive licensing requirements forced many libraries to cancel subscriptions and reduce their collections. Connected with this was another aspect, which up to this time had been exploited by the publishers, namely the practice of transferring the authors' rights completely to the publisher, who then had the exclusive rights for publication, distribution, translation, and reproduction.

As a result of this convention of transferring exclusive rights to the author's intellectual property to the publisher, the entire scientific community had made itself dependent on the publisher's publication strategy and pricing policy for the distribution of research results. Thus, a sort of 'grass roots' democracy movement developed among the authors and researchers who built up preprint servers based on the example of Paul Ginsparg, a physicist at the Los Alamos National Laboratory, who in 1991 started his preprint server for highenergy physics papers, to set up a forum for rapid dissemination of information. The concept of the preprint server as a 'correction' to the deficiencies of the commercial scientific publishing paradigm spread to other subject areas (psychology, economics, etc.) and various preprint servers sprang up round the world. The original high-energy physics preprint server ('LANL') has now moved with its originator to Cornell University and includes a much broader spectrum of pre- and e-print research results (http://arXiv.org). The impact of preprint servers is not just as a correction to the delays in commercial journal publishing, but also as a reflection of the philosophy of free access to information which has been promulgated by many proponents of full-text (e-print) servers. This has also 'scratched' the gloss of the peer-review mechanism which many commercial scientific journals use as justification for ever-increasing subscription prices.

The three aspects contributing to the development of the OAI – dissatisfaction with the previous, commercially dominated realm of scientific publishing and its delays; the rapidly expanding spectrum of digital library activities which included pre- and e-print servers; and the attempts to return authors' rights to the intellectual content back to the authors themselves instead of to third parties – still represent the basic hurdles and philosophical issues connected with the technical solutions. The free-access philosophy and the reform-oriented character surrounding the development of the OAI remain issues, but these cannot be solved by the operating structure of the OAI alone. Instead, the OAI has concentrated in the last two years on refining and testing the original premise for achieving interoperability and metadata standardization with a technical solution. This does not mean that the OAI is uninterested in the surrounding issues. In fact, as Cliff Lynch points out, many of the same people involved in the OAI are involved in other activities to reform the scientific communication model. However, the priority of the OAI over the last two years has been to achieve a firm basis for a simple, easy-toimplement technical specification and metadata standard that could first solve the technical issues of the interoperability of e-print servers.

The organization of the OAI The OAI evolved in

October 1999 after Paul Ginsparg, Richard Luce and Herbert van de Sompel (all at that time of the Los Alamos National Laboratory) invited a group of prominent researchers, computer scientists, and librarians involved in networked information research to Santa Fe, New Mexico, to examine the possibilities for establishing a 'universal service for nonpeer-reviewed scholarly literature' between various growing electronic full-text repositories serving different scholarly communities throughout the world. The goal of the meeting was to determine the technical and organizational requirements for creating a service which could search the metadata of all preprint servers regardless of discipline and connect all these servers into a virtual preprint server, thereby creating a new scholarly communication model. This group came to consensus on the aims and architecture of a metadata harvesting protocol and the basis of the metadata to be harvested. The Santa Fe group wanted a very simple, low-barrier-to-entry interface, and to shift implementation complexity and operational processing load away from the repositories and to the developers of federated search services, repository redistribution services and the like.

A technical specification entitled the 'Santa Fe Convention' defined a simple set of metadata deemed necessary for federated resource discovery in distributed full-text repositories and a prototype metadata harvester was developed shortly thereafter using the Dienst technology. For a short time between October 1999 and early 2000, this initiative was called the 'Universal Pre-Print Service' whereby the emphasis on preprints quickly changed to include the aspect of archiving (and author self-archiving) and just as rapidly to e-prints of all kinds. With the name change to 'Open Archives Initiative', a certain amount of controversy arose, associated with the two terms 'open' and 'archives' – whereby the issues of openness in the technical sense are not automatically seen as being equivalent to being without charge. Under the sponsorship and supporting guidance of the Digital Library Federation (DLF) and the Coalition of Networked Information (CNI), organizational structures for the OAI were introduced which are still basically in place: a Steering Committee of 12 persons representing digital library projects, scientific e-print servers, major academic and research libraries, and sponsoring agencies for networked information were formed to review policy and procedural issues surrounding the technical development and public aware- ness of the OAI Protocol for Metadata Harvesting. A Technical Committee, formed of computer scientists, systems specialists, and library systems developers, was brought together to test, revise, and enhance the original prototype metadata harvester protocol with further input from early adopters and the participants of several international workshops conducted in the context of various digital library events. As of the autumn of 2001, new members were integrated into the Technical Committee to reflect the greater scope of the application of the OAI-PMH in international projects and to evaluate the current technical approach, modifying it or enhancing it as deemed necessary.

Funding for the development of the OAIPMH was obtained from the US National Science Foundation (grant no. IIS-9817416) and the US Defense Advanced Research Projects Agency (DARPA) (contract no. N66001-98-1-8908). The Executive Office of the OAI was established at the Computer Science Department of Cornell University with Carl Lagoze and Herbert van de Sompel. Further support for the OAI executive office and the OAI organizational structure comes from the US Council for Library and Information Resources (CLIR) and the Coalition for Networked Information (CNI). Mailing lists for the two committees, as well as for implementors' groups and an OAIgeneral mailing list, are supported at Cornell University, as is the maintenance of the OAI Homepage (www.openarchives.org) and the online registry of OAI-

Data Repositories and Service Providers

CONCLUSION

Digital library initiatives in India are still in a promising stage of development. Many of the initiatives are one time projects with a limited grant, without proper planning for continuity. Important issues such as project objectives, preservation methods, content selection, and coordination with other similar initiatives, access mechanism, sustainability and cost factor should be addressed. The digital library concept in the Indian context is a new, that can become reality through projects and programmes funded by the government and the initiatives taken by the Libraries, which would like to develop a digital library, must make careful planning and undertake viability study, as digital library projects requires careful selection of hardware, software, materials and standards to be used in their preservation.

QUESTIONS

1. Define Open Archives Initiative (OAI)?
2. List out the Major digital Libraries Initiatives?
3. Define Problem of Digital Initiatives?
4. Define file format?

4

Building the Digital Library

INTRODUCTION

Computerisation of the library during past few decades has focused heavily on creation of surrogate records of printed documents available in a library or for providing computerised services through secondary databases held locally on CD-ROM or magnetic tapes. The integrated library packages have served well in providing access to documents at bibliographic level. Similarly, secondary services like MEDLINE, INSPEC, COMPENDEX plus and CAS have proved themselves as effective tools for bibliographic control of research information. However, since these databases provided only bibliographic information on research articles, users had to depend heavily on physical collection available either in their institutional library or on interlibrary loan from other libraries for references retrieved from the secondary services.

Attempts were made in past to make the full text of research articles available through online search services, although technology available till late 1980s and early 1990s supported only simple text (ASCII) without graphics. Tools, techniques and protocols necessary for building-up digital libraries evolved with availability of computing power that allows parallel processing, multitasking, parallel consultation and parallel knowledge navigation and software tools that facilitate artificial intelligence and interactivity. Coincided with the availability of software, hardware and networking technology, the advent of world wide web (WWW), its ever increasing usage and highly evolved browsers have paved the way for creation of digital libraries. With rapid developments in technologies necessary for developing digital libraries, the world of digital information resources has expanded quickly and exponentially.

OBJECTIVES

- To have a look for the current digitization status among the libraries.
- To evaluate the Open Source Software for digital libraries.
- To critically examine repository approaches towards collecting and disseminating non-formal electronic resources in digital library.

BUILDING THE DIGITAL LIBRARY

The most important component of a digital, library is the digital collection it holds or has access to. Viability and extent of usefulness of a digital library would depend upon the critical mass of digital collection it has. A digital library can have a wide range of resources. It may contain either paper-based conventional documents or information contained in computer-processible form. Information contents of a digital library, depending on the media type it contains, may include a combination of structured/ unstructured text, numerical data, scanned images. graphics, audio and video recordings. Different types of resources need to be handled differently in a digital library. us bridge'^ divided resources for a digital library in following four distinct categories, i.e., legacy, transition, new and future.

Legacy resources

These are largely non-digital resources, including manuscript, print, slides, maps, audio and video recordings. lnspite of the fact that large investments are being made in the process of digitisation of resources, vast majority of existing legacy resources will remain outside the electronic domain for many years to come. These legacy resources are the major resources of existing libraries

Transition resources

Primarily designed for another medium (mostly print), are those which are being or have been digitised, 6 making the transition into the digital world. Such resources are converted for increased access and to reduce reliance on physical libraries. The transition resources are either digitized images or images that are converted to text by the process of OCR.

New digital resources

These are either expressly created as digital or are created in parallel to print. Publishers are increasingly moving to XML or SGML format. These formats are used to generate data files required for producing printed outputs. The SGMUXML databases are also used for generating HTMLIPDFIXHTML or postscript file dynamically using appropriate DTDs. New digital resources are designed with a particular use in mind employing new Internet and web technologies embodying a great variation and value addition.

Future digital resources

There is an increasingly wide range of digital resources from formally published electronic journals and electronic books through databases and datasets in many formats, i. e., bibliographic, full text, image, audio, video, statistical and numeric datasets. Future resources may contain data sets which are not formally specified. A digital library is not a single entity although if may have digital contents created in-house or acquired in digital formats stored locally on servers. A digital library may also act as a portal site providing access to digital collections held elsewhere.

DIGITIZATION

Some materials in a digital library are 'born digital'; that is to say they were created, and are always used, in digital form. But much digital library content has to be created by a process of digitization. Digitization is converting print-on-paper resources to digital form, usually by scanning.

The Process

Digitizing information starts with images of pages, progresses through raw character recognizing to corrected text, and finishes with assigning descriptive data for easy retrieval. Each step provides more utility but at additional cost. (Berger, 1999)

Below are the steps to take when dealing with any information that is in hard copy. Born digital material is handled differently as it requires less work to add to the library's digital collection.

Document preparation

- remove pages from their bindings;
- trim each page so that no rough edges are left;
- mend rips and tears with acid-free binding tape;

Registering documents to keep track of them.

A record of the documents must be kept for reference whenever the need arises. The register helps to show who is handling what and how far the library has gone in the digitization project.

Scanning pages

To scan a document, place it face down on the scanner platen, or put the pages into the sheet feeder. If you have a sheet-fed scanner, cut the book open (easy and neat if you use a printer's cutting machine) to get individual sheets you can feed through the scanner. If necessary, you can rebind the books later.

Before scanning, the library has to set parameters to be applied on all the documents. This will ensure uniformity.

The scanner usually comes with software for converting image to text. This will help with the conversion from image to editable text.

Formatting and editing

The scanned image can be saved as a PDF (Portable Document Format) file using Adobe Acrobat; or GIF (Graphical Interchange Format) or JPEG (Joint Photographic Experts Group) file. The format of saving is determined at the planning stage. However most people prefer to save the images as JPEG since JPEG can be uploaded as HTML and furthermore, JPEG retains more information as it compresses an image. JSTOR uses GIF files to display the textual images.

Images should be scanned at the highest quality possible to not only have a good quality copy to archive, but also to ensure that with improvements in technology, the scanned copy would not become obsolete.

It is preferable to scan and save all documents first before embarking on the editing. A file structure should be created to save the images. Directories with their subdirectories should be set up for each series or volume of documents. For example, each page scanned can be named individually (i.e. Thes_12010-1p22), all pages in a document can be saved together in a folder (i.e. Th2010-1) and all issues would be saved together in a volume folder (i.e. Thes_1). This logical progression will make it possible to keep the order intact, even when an individual page is missing and has to be scanned at another time. The scanning should be in chronological order.

When editing images, blemishes must be removed from the pages, the height and width of the images have to be standardized and the images must be blurred or sharpened as necessary. Photo imaging software applications, such as Paint Shop Pro and some versions of Adobe Photoshop can be used to do this work.

Optical Character Recognition Software (OCR) is then used to edit text versions of the images. OCR is the process whereby a computer program "reads" the text from an image of a document and converts it into ASCII text. The use of optical character recognition is ideal as it converts scanned pages of text into electronic text, which enables full-text searching.

PDF files are favorable as most academic users are accustomed to them and already have Acrobat Reader; if not, the Reader is free and easy to install. Acrobat uses an efficient compression scheme and provides a user-friendly means of navigating through documents. It also automatically sizes each page for viewing and printing.

Creating a searchable database of the text, filing structure;

The structure of work involved in creating the searchable database will be determined by the DLMS that the library decides to adapt for its collection. Regardless of the system adapted, certain action must be taken in order to make the digital items searchable and accessible to the target audience.

For the digital content to be searchable, accurate metadata must be assigned to each item. The library must agree on the standards to use in this exercise. The digital content and meta-data about physical content must be contained, controlled, and understood in order for the basic functions of content management and content preservation to occur.

Metadata can be assigned at the point of editing and formatting or collectively afterwards. The order is determined by the staff beforehand. Creating searchable database of the digital content will then be possible once the metadata has been created.

Many institutions, including large universities, have created their own databases using such tools as SQL and MS Access. MySQL is an open source database that has become popular in nonprofit environments. Many libraries have also used FileMaker Pro, a cross-platform relational database application from FileMaker Inc.

FileMaker Pro and MS Access require experience with relational databases. They are not as scalable as SQL, i.e., they become sluggish and start to break down at about 70,000 records. FileMaker Pro is cross-platform, whereas MS Access works only in a PC environment.

PLANNING

Planning mainly involves identifying various tasks related to creating a digital library collection, developing strategies for handling these tasks, identifying required resources and formulating a timeline for accomplishing these tasks. If there is a need to have a large digital project, you may consider conducting a feasibility study to assess the viability of the project before detailed planning. The outcome of the feasibility study could be a formal proposal for obtaining management approval or grant for the project.

a. The first step in planning a digital library collection development project is to specify the need for creating the digital library collection, its purpose and target user community. You should indicate if management, the users or others have expressed this need and defined what this need is. The purpose could be improving preservation of some rare or delicate materials, improving access to and the visibility of certain material or facilitating re-use of documents. It is important to identify the target user community for a digital library collection and their profile

b. There is the need to define the source material that constitutes the digital library collections and the key attributes of this source material. Examples of source material include project reports, staff publications, working papers, theses, dissertation, audio and video lectures, songs and musical scores etc. There is also the need to specify what portion of the material is to be digitized and if all the material or only a sub-set will be covered in the digital collection. Remember to assess copyright restrictions.

c. Define the key features of the digital library collection you plan to build. Identify the nature of the collection e.g. static or dynamic. Indicate the type of usages you would allow the users to adhere to and the kind of service delivery they should expect from you e.g. CDROM or on-line or both. Define metadata, search and retrieval requirements.

d. The important task in creating a digital library collection is the conversion of the source materials available in hardcopy into a digital format. There should be a clear cut statement about the related requirements and their processes, namely:

   i. How to convert the source material into required digital format.

ii. What are the digitization requirements?

iii. The workflow involved in digitizing the source material.

e. Identify the resources and money required for creating and maintaining digital collections. There is a need to identify:

i. What type of information technology (IT) infrastructure is required for establishing and maintaining the digital collections?

ii. What are the personnel requirements and

iii. What are the financial requirements involve for setting up and maintaining the collection.

f. Finally, there is the need to define how the project is going to be implemented and what the major milestones and time requirements are?

IMPLEMENTATION

Planning is followed by implementation. That is getting down to the actual steps required to set up the collection. This means that there must be a need to obtain the management approval for the plan and the required resources before proceeding with the implementation. There is a need to identify and designate a project manager to lead the implementation of the digital project. For large digital library projects, it is essential to have a full time project manager for the project period.

The Implementation of a digital library project involves the following activities.

i. Establish the project team

ii. Set up the Information Technology (IT) infrastructure

iii. Procure and install digital library software

iv. Finalize policies and specifications

v. Complete arrangement of workflow for digitization

vi. Set up the digital library collection site in case of Internet distribution

vii. Obtain copyright permissions and

viii. Release the digital library collection for use.

Methods

Digitizing the text and other material, following four methods can be used.

(a) Manual data entry Scanning;

(b) Optical Character recognition (OCR);

(c) Excalibur Technologies and pattern recognition technologies;

(d) Document Imaging.

(a) The simplest method converting an image of a page (or the real page of text) into digital text is to enter it manually. This is usually a time consuming method but very useful from the point of view of information retrieval.

(b) In the second method, scanners are used to take digital pictures of objects. Scanners can be simple desk top machines or very large and complex systems that process thousands of documents.

(c) Another simple digitization process is of OCR i.e. scanning printed pages to build a digital database of text. This process uses OCR (Optical Character Recognition) software, which takes a picture of the page and then turns it into digital text, which can be edited or fully indexed. OCR software must distinguish between black and white areas of text.

(d) Excalibur Technologies and Pattern Recognition Technologies are the next generation of OCRs, represented by Pixie, a product being developed by Excalibur Technologies. This software uses a technology called Adaptive Pattern Recognition, which attempts to mimic aspects of the neural patterns of the brain. The software can be taught to recognize variations and relationships in pattern, such as patterns of text rather than readable text. The retrieval of search terms uses what Excalibur calls "fuzzy matching".

(e) Document Imaging, a simple method if capturing text, involves taking an electronic picture of each page of text with the same type of scanner as one would use for OCR. However, the difference is that the images are stored as graphic files rather than text files. A similar technology is used for fax transmission. Each page is stored as one picture. The text on the page cannot be edited or indexed.

INSTITUTIONAL REPOSITORIES

Repository and digital library are two terms that seem confusing to even academicians these days. The fact is that a repository is quite different from the digital library. Let's go through the main difference between these two in terms of storing contents or education materials. An institutional repository is an online storehouse for collecting, preserving, and disseminating digital copies of an institution, especially a research institution. It makes the intellectual output freely and openly available for an organisation or many institutes or just one section. On the other hand a digital library is mainly a gateway to electronic resources including e-books, e-journals, magazines, thesis, research papers, bibliographic databases and management tools.

A repository provides storage facility for library collections, but not access nor retrieval of information from persons, unless distribution of such collection is established by the proprietor of the information and the person in charge of the repository. Institutional repositories can be an archive of an institution's research collection. Institutional repositories can be considered as a set of services for the administration and dissemination of digital materials developed by the organisation and its members. Of course it essential for the organisation to the safeguard these digital materials, including long-term preservation along with access or distribution.

Digital library is a special electronic library with huge storage capacity for the collection of digital objects that can include text, animation, audio visual materials, in electronic media formats. It provides means for organizing, storing, and retrieving the files and media contained in the library collection. Digital libraries can differ hugely in size and scope, and can be administered by individuals, organisations, or established physical libraries of an establishment or academic institutions. Besides, the digital resources can be stored locally, or accessed remotely via computer networks.

Digital library software available nowadays is helpful for the easy management and retrieval of contents in and out of an organization. It provides a new way of organizing information and publishing it online or offline. It helps to empower users, particularly in universities, libraries, and other public service institutions, to create their own digital libraries. Digital libraries radically reform the way of information dissemination and knowledge acquisition in the fields of education, science and culture around the world.

In short, we can say that institutional repositories depend upon the voluntary contribution of contents provided by scholars/authors while Digital Library is the product of deliberate data collection and development policy. Institutional Repositories are mainly sources that offer limited user services while digital library are typically designed to preserve and retrieve the contents for various purposes including reading, research etc.

Role Do Institutional Repositories

While institutional digital libraries are making inroads into the consciousness of their users, it is nevertheless true that the march of digital content via the Web makes many of their services less vital than they were, and even redundant to a growing proportion of users on campus. The concept of institutionality is an increasingly fragile one when we consider digital content and digital libraries, and we, therefore, must ask whether we should be developing institutional repositories at all. Are they an attempt to shut the stable door after the horse has bolted? All institutional digital library services face a tough battle in being accepted on campuses because alternative systems usually exist, and their shortcomings are not always obvious. Institutional repositories are not an intuitively necessary development in the minds of most academics. Few people yet feel they do not need a physical library on their campus doorstep, but many – particularly those experienced in using subject-based repositories such as arXiv – are surprised to hear librarians arguing for the creation of institutional repositories as new services.

Might it not be better for publishing agencies – content aggregators – to work on behalf of subject disciplines directly in the development both of repositories and broader digital libraries, with institutional digital libraries requiring only a minimal presence? After all, repository and digital library development to date has been more successful in the disciplinary than the institutional sphere, and has been driven directly by academics themselves. Libraries, by trying to create generalised institutional services, are confronted by the twin difficulties of acting as third-party agents between academics and their content and so being perceived as unnecessary, and of seeking to impose conditions upon academics in order to attract content, which may be resented.

It is not yet clear whether institutional repositories will take root and flourish in the digital knowledge landscape. As an innovation, they are still at an early stage of diffusion. What is clear is that they are regarded as a strong and important new idea by many organisations which are concerned with the dissemination of research outputs. Their appeal lies in the idea of 'groundedness'. Institutions are themselves the ground from which emerge the outputs of research – ideas, proposals, hypotheses, experiments, data and reported results. These outputs now share a common DNA in digital representation. It is this common base format which allows institutions to look more closely at their traditional way of managing research outputs – using print and microform – in order to discover whether there are new and more efficient modes of operation. 'Research outputs' traditionally are just that – research publications which are 'put out', given away to third parties for further processing. In such a process there is a loss of control, by the institution and the research funder, and with that loss of control come the problems which libraries are well aware of, as are increasing numbers of academic staff and researchers: the loss of the alignment of the output with the aims of the research funder; and the partial loss of the output to research generally across the world, because publishers require payment for their efforts in dissemination. The outputs, now in the hands of publishers, have to be 'bought back'. Inevitably, this means that only some researchers will benefit. But if the outputs are of near-publication quality while still 'on the ground', because of their digital DNA, then what new opportunities are opened up?

In pre-digital times, when researchers wrote up their results for publication, they would have been posted, hand-written or in typescript, to a publisher – the only agent with the technology to present the finished paper in a pleasing form, and to reproduce it in multiples sufficient to meet the likely demand across the world, in their journals. Publishers also managed a third very important process – that of verification that the research was of a quality which made it valuable to other researchers. This is achieved by the system of peer review, and is critical to the advancement of knowledge, and, therefore, to the careers of researchers as they develop. If a piece of research is flawed or unoriginal, then the advancement of knowledge is stultified or even damaged, and at some future point this fact is likely to become obvious to other researchers, so that the researcher responsible is tarnished in the eyes of their peers – with obvious consequences for personal self-esteem and career development.

In the digital age, the presentation and reproduction functions do not require the intermediation of a publisher. This is what an institutional repository can do. In doing so, the institution is granted a capture function similar to the archival functions which have long existed – in pre-digital time also – for corporate records. Sending research papers to publishers immediately they have been written was a necessary process, but not an ideal one. If the overall work required is not made noticeably more arduous, how much better to record the outflow of the institution's research as it leaves the premises, stamping it at source with the institution's imprimatur, and asserting ownership rights over it – either for the institution or for the author themselves. In the words of Herbert Van de Sompel, 'Scholars deserve an innately digital scholarly communication system that is able to capture the digital scholarly record, make it accessible, and preserve it over time' (Van de Sompel et al., 2004). Van de Sompel's analysis is founded on a concern about data loss and the need to provide effective data curation, but it implies an emphasis on the role of the institution in the lifecycle nonetheless:

> We feel this loss needs to be remedied in a future scholarly communication system by natively embedding the capability to record and expose such dynamics, relationships, and interactions in the scholarly communication infrastructure. Recording this body of information is synonymous to recording the evolution of

scholarship at a fine granularity. This will allow tracing the origins of specific ideas to their roots, analyzing trends at a specific moment in time, and forecasting future research directions. (Ibid)

This new functionality is obviously desirable but was given little attention in the past because it was virtually impossible to administer, and there was no obvious benefit in any case. Institutional repositories now make the administration relatively simple, and the future benefits have come dramatically into focus in recent times. These benefits derive mainly from the extraordinary potential of repository networking which has been made possible through the development of the OAI-PMH protocol.

Herbert Van de Sompel, developer of OAI-PMH, has regularly described how the invention has the ability to serve the purposes of the academy – and the interested public – without sacrificing any of the tried and trusted elements of the research dissemination and publication process. He quotes the scholarly communication lifecycle model of Roosendal and Guertz, with its five key components (Roosendaal and Guertz, 1997):

Registration : allows claims of precedence for a scholarly finding.

Certification : establishes the validity of a registered scholarly claim.

Awareness : allows actors in the scholarly system to remain aware of new claims and findings.

Archiving : preserves the scholarly record over time.

Rewarding : rewards actors for their performance in the communication system based on metrics derived from that system.

In the traditional print world, registration and certification require publishers, and awareness and archiving are carried out by libraries. Rewarding is done by a variety of actors, both institutional (e.g. promotion by the university) and at national and international levels, through rewards such as increased funding for research, visiting professorships, and invitations to contribute to scholarly works and conferences. In what Van de Sompel elsewhere describes as a 'decomposed scholarly communication system' (Van de Sompel, 2000) involving repositories on the Web, there is no longer a need for separate agents responsible for each stage in the process. Instead, the repository, working in concert with other compliant repositories across the Web, becomes an 'interoperable grid' supplying in itself all of the elements of the system – registration, certification, awareness, archiving and rewarding.

Van de Sompel also presents librarians with some serious food for thought. The migration of the scholarly process onto the Web, with a central role for the institutional repository, raises questions about the continued role of the library as an agent for the purchase of published material:

It has become increasingly difficult for libraries to fulfil their fundamental role of safeguarding equity of access. At the core of the problems that libraries are facing is the total dependency on information held upstream in the information chain. (Van de Sompel, 2000)

In other words, they are in danger of becoming redundant – in at least those of their functions which depend on content held elsewhere. But there is some good news for libraries if they can seize the initiative presented by institutional repositories and ensure that they run them on behalf of their organisations. Libraries are close to authors, and so in 'a great position to fulfil the registration function i.e., obtain institutional material.' They are also clearly well qualified to archive this material. They are 'fast at embracing new technologies', and full of very knowledgeable people. However, there are some dread warnings as well:

As organizations libraries are slow movers, hosted by slowly moving institutions. Libraries are slow to recognize the fact that a new technology may allow [or beg] for a new mode of operation. The information world runs on Internet time (Van de Sompel, 2000)

This slow speed of response might be fatal for libraries. They may have the technology at an early stage, but they generally do not use it to engender change in their host institution's organisational practices, and so they run the risk of losing out to other players in the digital content marketplace. The greatest challenges of all for university libraries wishing to populate institutional repositories within their digital libraries may, therefore, be outreach and liaison. These are not activities which are normally given high priority, and this must change if libraries are to claim a key role in the scholarly communication lifecycle.

OPEN SOURCE SOFTWARE FOR DIGITAL LIBRARIES

Open source defines method of software development, that harnesses the power of distributed peer review and transparency of progress. This technique helps to provide better quality software's having higher reliability, flexibility with lower cost, and an end to the traditional vendor lock-in. The source code and rights that where normally reserved for copyright holders are now being provided under a free software license that permits developers / users to study, change, improve and at times also to distribute the software.

Digital library refers to a collection that constitutes electronic resources, accessible through the World Wide Web. It often contains electronic versions of books, photographs, videos that are owned by a "physical" library. Open source digital library software presents a system for the construction and presentation of information collections. It helps in building collections with searching and metadata-bases browsing facilities. Moreover, they are easily maintained and can be augmented and rebuilt automatically. With many Open Source Software (OSS) applications now available for library and information management, Organizations now have novel options for acquiring and implementing systems. The Open Source Software applications for library and Information management that will be discussed in this paper are:

- DSpace
- Greenstone
- EPrints

DIGITAL LIBRARY MANAGEMENT SYSTEMS

Digital Libraries have greatly evolved during the last few years. They are no longer only the digital counter part of physical libraries (or physical museums, video achieves, etc.) rather they are intricate networked systems capable of supporting communication and collaboration among different, worldwide distributed user communities. Digital Library management system evolved with the inception of Digital Library. Digital Library management system provides the appropriate framework both for the production and administration of Digital Library System by incorporating functionality essentially fundamental to Digital Libraries, and also provides provision for integration of additional software that provides more refined and advanced functionality. Digital Library can thus be established by setting up and deploying a Digital Library Management System and then loading or harvesting content. This approach largely simplifies and reduces the effort required to set up a Digital Library that promises a guaranteed better quality of service. These generic systems have started to appear from the second half of 1990's even though implementing the devised DLMS features only to some extent. The major characteristics that distinguish them from each other are the class of functionality offered, the type of object model for information being supported, and the openness of their architecture's. The DLMS (Digital Library Management System) available are commercial as well as open source.

But, Open Source DLMS's (Digital Library Management System) are the one that will be studied. Open source digital library management software's provide extensible features to administrators' and allows an organization to showcase their digital achieve to world audience. With full rights of software available under GPL and source code being provided with the software, Organization's can extend the functionality of the software as being required for the particular operation. The DLMS' (Digital Library Management System) studied are:

1. DSpace : The DSpace is a joint project of the MIT Libraries and HP labs. It is a digital asset management system that allows institutions, such as libraries to collect, archive, index, and disseminate the scholarly and intellectual efforts of a community. Written with a combination of technologies by MIT, it is primarily used to capture bibliographic information describing articles, papers, theses, and dissertations. DSpace is adaptable to different community needs. Interoperability between systems is built-in and it adheres to international standards for metadata format. Being an open source technology platform, DSpace can be customized to extend its capabilities. Some of its characteristics as shown in DSpace documentation are as:

(a) It is a service model for open access and/or digital archiving for perennial access.

(b) Provides a platform to frame an Institutional Repository and the collections are searchable and retrievable by the Web.

(c) Helps to make available institution-based scholarly material in digital formats. The collections will be open and interoperable.

The organization of data modal in DSpace is intended to mirror the structure of the organization using the DSpace. Each DSpace site is divided into communities, which can be further divided into sub-communities reflecting the typical university structure of college, department, research centre, or laboratory. Communities contain collections, which are groupings of related content. A collection may appear in more than one community. Each collection is composed of items, which are the basic archival elements of the archive. Each item is owned by one collection. Additionally, an item may appear in additional collections; however every item has one and only one owning collection. Items are further subdivided into named bundles of bitstreams. Bitstreams are, as the name suggests, streams of bits, usually ordinary computer files. Bitstreams that are somehow closely related (for example HTML files and images that compose a single HTML document) are organized into bundles.

As specified by Robert Tansley, Mick Bass, Margret Branschofsky, Grace Carpenter, Greg McClellan, David Stuve (05-Oct-2005) the bundles most items tend to have included the following:

(a) ORIGINAL : The bundle contains the original, deposited bitstreams.

(b) THUMBNAILS: Thumbnails of any image bitstreams.

(c) TEXT : It includes extracted full-text from bitstreams in ORIGINAL, for indexing.

(d) LICENSE: It contains the deposit license that the submitter granted the host organization; putting it differently it specifies the rights that the hosting organizations have.

(e) CC_LICENSE: It contains the distribution license, if any (a Creative Commons license) associated with the item. This license specifies what end users can do with the downloaded content.

Each bitstream is associated with one Bitstream Format. Because preservation services are an important aspect of the DSpace service, it is important to capture the specific formats of files that users submit. The format of bitstream is a unique and provides a coherent way to sort out a particular file format. The implicit or explicit notion of a bitstream format is to provide means how material in that format can be interpreted. For example, the bitstream interpretation for still images compression encoded in the JPEG standard is defined explicitly in the Standard ISO/IEC10918-1.

In DSpace data modal each item has one qualified Dublin Core metadata record. An item may have other metadata stored in as serialized bitstream, but for every time Dublin Core is used to provide interoperability and ease of discovery. The Dublin Core may be entered by end-users as they submit content, or it might be derived from other metadata as part of an ingest process. The removal of items in DSpace is done in two ways: They may be 'withdrawn', which means they remain in the archive but are completely hidden from view. In this case, if an end-user attempts to access the withdrawn item, they are presented with a 'tombstone,' that indicates the item has been removed. For whatever reason, an item may also be 'expunged' if necessary, in which case all traces of it are removed from the archive. The features of DSpace as Digital Management Software are as follows:

(a) Authentication : DSpace allows contributors to limit access to items in DSpace, at both the collection and the individual item level. The mechanism whereby the system securely identifies its users.

(b) Authorization : The mechanism by which a DSpace determines what level of access a particular authenticated user should have to secure resources controlled by the system is done by keeping access control policies that allow it to understand what credentials are required (if any) to undertake particular actions upon particular resources. Authentication is provided through user passwords, X509 certificates or LDAP. Access controls can be administered by only authorized users. The access controls specify default distribution policy for all items, specify users to submit to collection and specify reviewers, approvers, and metadata editors for a collection's submission process. There are two built-in groups: 'Administrators', who can do anything in a site, and 'Anonymous', which is a list that contains all users. Assigning a policy for an action on an object to anonymous means giving everyone permission to do that action. (For example, most objects in DSpace sites have a policy of 'anonymous' READ.) Permissions must be explicit - lack of an explicit permission results in the default policy of 'deny'. Permissions also do not 'commute'; for example, if an e-person has READ permission on an item, they might not necessarily have READ permission on the bundles and bitstreams in that item. Currently Collections, Communities and Items are discoverable in the browse and search systems regardless of READ authorization.

(c) Non-dynamic HTML document Support : As mentioned by Tansley R, et al (2005) in the documentation, DSpace simply supports uploading and downloading of bitstreams as-is. This mechanism is good for majority of file –formats like PDF, Word Document and so on. As far as HTML documents are concerned they are complicated in the sense they consist of several files and are cross-linked with each other. This has important ramifications when it comes to digital preservation. Web pages also link to or include content from other sites, often imperceptibly to the end-user. Thus, in a few year's time, when someone views the preserved Web site, they will probably find that many links are now broken or refer to other sites than are now out of context. In fact, it may be unclear to an end-user when they are viewing content stored in DSpace and when they are seeing content included from another site, or have navigated to a page that is not stored in DSpace. This problem can manifest when a submitter uploads some HTML content. For example, the HTML document may include an image from an external Web site, or even their local hard drive. When the submitter views the HTML in DSpace, their browser is able to use the reference in the HTML to retrieve the appropriate image, and so to the submitter, the whole HTML document appears to have been deposited correctly. However, later on, when another user tries to view that HTML, their browser might not be able to retrieve the included image since it may have been removed from the external server. Hence the HTML will seem broken. There is much research going on the issues above. Currently, DSpace bites off a small, tractable chunk of this problem. DSpace can store and provide on-line browsing capability for self-contained, non-dynamic HTML documents. By dynamic content means no CGI script and so on. The links preserved for images, videos etc are preserved as relative links. Any absolute link is stored as is and will continue to link the source as long as it is live, and will eventually change or disappear.

(d) OAI-PMH Support : The OAI_PMH is a protocol for metadata harvesting. This allows sites to programmatically retrieve or 'harvest' the metadata from several sources, and offer services using that metadata, such as indexing or linking services. DSpace exposes the Dublin Core metadata for items that are publicly (anonymously) accessible. Additionally, the collection structure is also exposed via the OAI protocol's 'sets' mechanism. OCLC's open source OAICat framework is used to provide this functionality. The OAI service can also be configured to make use of any crosswalk plug-in to offer additional metadata formats, such as MODS. Deletion information for withdrawn items is not displayed by DSpace's OAI. DSpace also supports OAI-PMH resumption tokens. Hierarchy to manage contents (i.e. Communities, Collections, and Items).

(e) Object Management : The process of item ingestion in DSpace is via a web interface or batch item importer. In workflow process for item submission will initiate depending on the configuration of collection. The workflow process may contain one or more steps as per the user need. The collection and communities in DSpace are created via web interface.

(f) Import & Export : Import & Export for Communities, Collections and Items is supported by DSpace. It also includes batch tools to import and export items in a simple directory structure, where the Dublin Core metadata is stored in an XML file. This may be used as the basis for moving content between DSpace and other systems.

(g) Statistics : Statistics are provided for administrative usage. Statistical reports/summary can be used for performing analysis on repository, providing information like number of items uploaded, searched, number of epeople registered with the system etc.

(h) Handle System : To help in creation of persistent identifier for every item DSpace makes use of Handle system's global resolution feature. DSpace requires a storage and location independent mechanism for creating and maintaining identifiers. DSpace uses the CNRI Handle System for creating these identifiers. A Handle server runs as a separate process that receives TCP requests from other Handle servers, and issues resolution requests to a global server or servers if a Handle entered locally does not correspond to some local content.

(i) Customization & types of document supported: DSpace allows customization to accommodate the multidisciplinary and organizational needs of a large institution. Albeit DSpace provides a flexible data object modal. It does not allow construction of very different objects with independent metadata sets due to its database oriented architecture. DSpace allows minor intervention of user interface. DSpace collections include audio, video or text depending on the organizational needs. The system can function with many file types, including: PDF, HTML, JPEG, TIFF, MP3, and AVI etc.

(j) Standards Compliance : The default configuration permits DSpace to store metadata of an item in the Dublin Core Metadata Schema. This ensures that data can be exchanged with other standards compliant system, such as MARC21. MARC is an acronym for Machine-Readable Cataloguing.

(k) Optimized Search & Browse : As per Bass, M J et al (n.d), the system allows end-users to discover content in a number of ways, including:

- By default indexing of basic metadata set qualified DC is provided by DSpace. While as indexing of other metadata sets is provided by Jakarta Lucene search engine. Apache Lucene is written in java and provides high-performance, full-featured text search engine library. It provides technology for any application that requires full-text search, especially cross-platform (Lucene, 2012). Lucene supports fielded search, stemming & stop words removal. By default Browsing in DSpace is by title, author, and date field.
- Via external reference, such as a CNRI Handle. A persistent identifier used for every bitstreams of every item.

2. GREENSTONE

Greenstone Digital Library Software is a project from New Zealand that provides a new way of organizing information and making it available over the Internet. Collections of information comprise large numbers of documents (typically several thousand to several million), and a uniform interface is provided to them. Libraries include many collections, individually organized, though bearing a strong family resemblance. A configuration file determines the structure of a collection. Existing collections range from newspaper articles to technical documents, from educational journals to oral history, from visual art to videos, from MIDI pop music collections to ethnic folksongs.

A typical digital library built with Greenstone will contain many collections, individually organized. Easily maintained, collections can be augmented and rebuilt automatically. There are several ways to find information in most Greenstone collections. For example, you can search for particular words that appear in the text, or within a section of a document. Word search is provided as Greenstone constructs full-text indexes from the document text that is, indexes that enable searching on any words in the full text of the document. Indexes can be searched for particular words, combinations of words, or phrases, and results are ordered according to how relevant they are to the query. In most collections, descriptive data such as author, title, date, keywords, and so on, is associated with each document. This information is called metadata. Many document collections also contain full-text indexes of certain kinds of metadata. You can browse documents by title: just click on a book to read it. You can browse documents by subject. Subjects are represented by bookshelves: just click on a bookshelf to look at the books. Where appropriate, documents come complete with a table of contents: you can click on a chapter or subsection to open it, expand the full table of contents, or expand the full document into your browser window.

Collections can contain text, pictures, audio and video. Nontextual material is either linked into the textual documents or accompanied by textual descriptions such as figure captions to allow full-text searching and browsing [18]. Unicode is used throughout Greenstone. This allows any language to be processed and displayed in a consistent manner. Multilingual collections embody automatic language recognition, and the interface is available in all the major languages.

Before going online, these collections undergo the importing and building processes. First, documents, shown at the bottom of the figure, are imported into the XML-compliant Greenstone Archive Format. Then the archive files are built into various searchable indexes and a collection information database that includes the hierarchical structures that support browsing. When this is done, the collection is ready to go online and respond to requests for information.

Two components are central to the design of the runtime system: "receptionists" and "collection servers." From a user's point of view, a receptionist is the point of contact with the digital library. It accepts user input, typically in the form of keyboard entry and mouse clicks; analyzes it; and then dispatches a request to the appropriate collection server (or servers).This locates the requested piece of information and returns it to the receptionist for presentation to the user. Collection servers act as an abstract mechanism that handles the content of the collection, while receptionists are responsible for the user interface. Receptionists communicate with collection servers using a defined protocol. The implementation of this protocol depends on the computer configuration on which the digital library system is running. The most common case, and the simplest, is when there is one receptionist and one collection server, and both run on the same computer. This is what you get when you install the default Greenstone.

Collections are accessed over the Internet or published, in precisely the same form, on a self-installing Windows CDROM. Compression is used to compact the text and indexes. A Corba protocol supports distributed collections and graphical query interfaces. Listed below are some of special features possessed by the Greenstone:

(a) Accessible via web browser : Collections are accessed through a standard web browser (Netscape or

Internet Explorer) and combine easy-to-use browsing with powerful search facilities.

(b) Full Text and Field Search : The user can search the full text of the documents, or choose between indexes built from different parts of the documents. For example, some collections have an index of full documents, an index of sections, an index of titles, and an index of authors, each of which can be searched for particular words or phrases. Results can be ranked by relevance or sorted by a metadata element.

(c) Flexible browsing facilities : The user can browse lists of authors, lists of titles, lists of dates, classification structures, and so on. Different collections may offer different browsing facilities and even within a collection, a broad variety of browsing interfaces are available. Browsing and searching interfaces are constructed during the building process, according to collection configuration information.

(d) Create access structures automatically : The Greenstone software creates information collections that are very easy to maintain. All searching and browsing structures are built directly from the documents themselves. No links are inserted by hand, but existing links in originals are maintained. This means that if new documents in the same format become available, they can be merged into the collection automatically. Indeed, for some collections this is done by processes that wake up regularly, scout for new material, and rebuild the indexes—all without manual intervention.

(e) Make use of available metadata : Metadata, which is descriptive information such as author, title, date, keywords, and so on, may be associated with each document, or with individual sections within documents. Metadata is used as the raw material for browsing indexes. It must be either provided explicitly or derivable automatically from the source documents. The Dublin

Core metadata scheme is used for most electronic documents; however, provision is made for other schemes.

(f) Plug-in extends system's capabilities : In order to accommodate different kinds of source document, the software is organized in such a way that "plug-in" can be written for new document types. Plug-in currently exist for plain text, html, Word, PDF, PostScript, E-mail, some proprietary formats, and for recursively traversing directory structures and compressed archives containing such documents.

(g) Customization : The Greenstone allows customization of presentation of collection that are based on Extensible Style sheet Language transformation (XSLT) and other agents that govern the definite functions of Digital library. The architecture of Greenstone purvey:

i. A back end that provide services to manage documents and collections.

ii. A front end that provides a web based interface for searching and presentation of documents, collections.

(h) Designed for Multi-gigabyte collection : Collections can contain millions of documents, making the Greenstone system suitable for collections up to several gigabytes.

(i) Multilingual Support : Unicode is used throughout the software, allowing any language to be processed in a consistent manner. To date, collections have been built containing French, Spanish, Maori, Chinese, Arabic and English. On-the-fly conversion is used to convert from Unicode to an alphabet supported by the user's web browser.

(j) Collections support multiple formats : Greenstone collections can contain text, pictures, audio and video clips. Most non-textual material is either linked in to the textual documents or accompanied by textual descriptions (such as figure captions) to allow full-text searching and browsing.

(k) Administrative function provided : An "administrative" function enables specified users to authorize new users to build collections, protect documents so that they can only be accessed by registered users on presentation of a password, examine the composition of all collections, and so on. Logs of user activity can record all queries made to every Greenstone collection.

(l) Collections can be published on the Internet or on CD-ROM : The software can be used to serve collections over the World-Wide Web. Greenstone collections can be made available, in precisely the same form, on CDROM . The user interface is through a standard web browser (Netscape is provided on each disk), and the interaction is identical to accessing the collection on the web—except that response times are more predictable. The CD-ROMs run under all versions of the Windows operating system.

3. EPRINTS

EPrints is free software developed by the "University of Southampton, England". EPrints repository collects preserves and disseminates in digital format the research output created by a research community. It enables the community to deposit their preprints; post prints and other scholarly publications using a web interface, and organizes these publications for easy retrieval. It is the world's first, most widely used, and by far the most functional of all the available OA IR software's. It is created for and specifically focused on OA functionality. EPrints is an extensible content management system. It has been extensively configured to accommodate the needs of academics and researchers amid at dissemination and reporting, but it could be easily used for other things such as images, research data, audio archives - anything that can be stored digitally, but you'll have make more changes to the configuration. EPrints is OAI-complaint. It is highly configurable to achieve diverse needs, built on a coding platform that is amendable to rapid development.

The real strength of EPrints lies in its ease of use for both endusers and administrators. Submitting documents in EPrints is very straightforward. Users are taken through the submission process one step at a time and asked to provide metadata information along with an electronic copy of the document. Users can simply enter metadata such as document type, title, author name, date, etc. via a web form, no knowledge of HTML or XML is required. The metadata fields that appear on the form are selected by the administrator. Administrators can easily customize the metadata form, so that only those fields that are pertinent to a given collection are presented to the end-user. Submissions to achieve can be easily managed by the user, and also editing, updating, and removal of documents is possible after submission (although the administrator can limit these functions). Browsing in EPrints can be done based on any of the metadata fields within a collection, and multiple browsing criteria can be used. For example, in browsing a collection of theses, it would be possible to browse by department and then break down the results by supervisor and year. The browsing categories that are made available to the user are controlled by the administrator. EPrints build and manage OAI-compliant EPrints archives. The documents in an EPrints archive can be indexed to allow retrieval by online search engines like Google, which helps to ensure greater access to, and greater dissemination of any items uploaded to the archive. Searching is fairly limited in EPrints. As mentioned earlier, Boolean searching is not supported. It is also quite easy to run a search that yields no results. For end users accustomed to modern search engines and databases it might be discouraging to get an unsuccessful search with no suggestions for alternative search strategies.

In EPrints there is no such strict structural division into sections and collections that are still playing an important role, for example, to narrow the search to the repository. The idea is that all records are equivalent and do not form a hierarchy. Nevertheless, the hierarchy is needed to navigate through the repository, since the users can not exactly know the purpose of their search, having only a rough idea about it. The way to generate the navigation of any desired type using the related elements of the metadata fields, i.e. In EPrints the problem is solved using the so-called representations (views). A way to generate the navigation of any desired type using the related elements of the metadata fields, i.e. representation can be carried out on parts of the organization or by the author, or a more complex version, the year of publication, and then by Type, etc. Thus, in the EPrints data model it is possible to ensure flexible support to the hierarchical subject classification (according to silence, classification of the library of congress) and the tree of the subdivisions of organization. Such objects, as element, collection of files, file, are similar to the analogous into DSpace. Element is also the fundamental unit of storage and contains all metadata, allowed for the external use. The hierarchical structure of elements is significantly different. DSpace uses a more rigid system, although it covers most of the needs of the repository. EPrints allows you to create a more complex hierarchy based on different external representations.

Listed below are some of special features possessed by the EPrints:

(a) Accessibility via web browser : EPrints provides web based interface that makes it easy to use and administer.

(b) Full Text and Field Search : Searching is based on metadata not full text based search is supported by EPrints. Searching in EPrints allows scanning each of the metadata field types in the database by using simple or advanced search. Any metadata field can be searched with fine granularity by SQL querying the database.

(c) Administrative function provided : EPrints archive can use any metadata schema as being provided by the administrator. The administrator decides what metadata fields are held about each EPrints item. This is specified in three or four stages:

a. Definition of a maximal set of metadata fields that should be stored (e.g. authors, title, journal, journal volume, etc.).
b. Definition of different types of EPrints (e.g. refereed journal article, thesis, technical report, unpublished preprint, etc.).
c. Specification for each type which metadata fields should be stored, and which of those fields are mandatory.
d. Decide how these metadata fields should be projected into the Open Archives world. (If necessary, interoperability can be switched off, but this is strongly discouraged.)

(d) Open Source Software : EPrints uses traditional technologies and runs on pure Open Source systems. It uses MySQL, Apache database and web server. MySQL is the world's most popular open source database, recognized for its speed and reliability and Apache has been the most popular web server on the Internet since April of 1996.Eprints is programmed by using the script language "Perl", that is low level but powerful.

(e) Three user roles : administrator, editor and author.

a. Administrator role controls all back-end options such as organization of records, web interface appearance and functionality, and all other server-side settings.
b. Editor role reviews submissions before they are published online and may edit metadata on

submissions to maintain consistency or correct errors.

c. Author role allows submission of documents and management of previously submitted documents.

(f) OAI-PMH Support : EAS is fully interoperable with OAI (Open Archives Initiative) Protocol for Metadata Harvesting. Open Archives protocol allows sites to programmatically retrieve or 'harvest' the metadata from several sources, and offer services using that metadata, such as indexing or linking services. Such a service allows e-prints servers create the potential for a global network of cross-searchable research information, by allowing the contents of servers around the world searched simultaneously by using the OAI (Open Archives Initiative) protocol.

(g) Multilingual Support : Unicode is used throughout the software, allowing any language to be processed in a consistent manner.

(h) File formats supported : Functions with many file types, including: PDF, HTML, JPEG, TIFF, MP3, and AVI etc. Metadata schema can be tailored to meet the requirements.

(i) Statistics : Statistics are provided for administrative usage .Statistical reports/summary can be used for performing analysis on repository.

(j) Customization : The EPrints data modal consist of user defined metadata. In order to export data in other formats plug-ins can be written. For developers who wish to access the core Digital Library functionality Core API in Perl language is provided.

(k) Item preview in EPrints : Thumbnail preview of documents and images is generated automatically upon file upload.

STORAGE

Many organizations and owners of private collections

at least have some basic type of backup for their libraries. In some cases, this backup may take the form of simple scans, which might have been used to prove that certain literary works were actually part of a given collection for insurance purposes.

With so many affordable data storage systems available in today's marketplace, there's no reason to rely on scans as your sole means of backing up your collection. Remember – physical scans are just as susceptible to physical threats that can destroy them as the materials in your collection are.

If you're going to limit the number of people who can access your library to local or in-house users, you may want to consider physically backing up your collection with servers. Flash and hybrid data storage solutions may also work for your purposes.

If you want your library to be accessible to a wider audience all over the country or throughout the world, there is another data storage technology you should consider. And it's the cloud.

Here are some of the benefits that cloud storage can provide:

Security : Cloud storage protects your collection from physical threats because your data is stored in the cloud, not a tangible space. It also keeps your library safe from digital threats with frequent security updates to guard against cyber-attacks and hackers.

Easy Recovery : When you use paid cloud storage for your library, you're not relying on a physical device to store your data. Even if your archives and servers are leveled in a fire, you will still be able to access your library when it's stored in the cloud because calamities that cause physical damage in the "real" world don't impact data that's stored in the cloud.

Accessibility : With cloud data storage, anyone with the appropriate credentials can access your library from any location using just about any kind of device that can connect to the Internet.

Searchable : Depending on the type of cloud storage you choose, users may also be able to browse your collection and search it as if it's a virtual library. If your library is often used for research, the ability to search your collection can be a significant benefit.

ARCHIVES

Physical archives differ from physical libraries in several ways. Traditionally, archives are defined as:

1. Containing primary sources of information (typically letters and papers directly produced by an individual or organization) rather than the secondary sources found in a library (books, periodicals, etc.).
2. Having their contents organized in groups rather than individual items.
3. Having unique contents.

The technology used to create digital libraries is even more revolutionary for archives since it breaks down the second and third of these general rules. In other words, "digital archives" or "online archives" will still generally contain primary sources, but they are likely to be described individually rather than (or in addition to) in groups or collections. Further, because they are digital, their contents are easily reproducible and may indeed have been reproduced from elsewhere. The Oxford Text Archive is generally considered to be the oldest digital archive of academic physical primary source materials.

Archives differ from libraries in the nature of the materials held. Libraries collect individual published books and serials, or bounded sets of individual items. The books and journals held by libraries are not unique, since multiple copies exist and any given copy will generally prove as satisfactory as any other copy. The material in archives and manuscript libraries are "the unique records of corporate bodies and the papers of individuals and families"

A fundamental characteristic of archives is that they have to keep the context in which their records have been created and the network of relationships between them in order to preserve their informative content and provide understandable and useful information over time. The fundamental characteristic of archives resides in their hierarchical organization expressing the context by means of the archival bond. Archival descriptions are the fundamental means to describe, understand, retrieve and access archival material. At the digital level, archival descriptions are usually encoded by means of the Encoded Archival Description XML format. The EAD is a standardized electronic representation of archival description which makes it possible to provide union access to detailed archival descriptions and resources in repositories distributed throughout the world.

Given the importance of archives, a dedicated formal model, called Nested Sets for Object Hierarchies (NESTOR) built around their peculiar constituents, has been defined. NESTOR is based on the idea of expressing the hierarchical relationships between objects through the inclusion property between sets, in contrast to the binary relation between nodes exploited by the tree. NESTOR has been used to formally extend the 5S model to define a digital archive as a specific case of digital library able to take into consideration the peculiar features of archives.

PRESERVING DIGITAL COLLECTION

Digital preservation represents an emergent area of digital library research and practice. It focuses on the policies, technologies, and strategies to ensure that digital library objects and collections are available and usable now and in the future. Digital preservation encompasses materials born in the digital format as well as those converted from the analog format through the digitization process. Concerns about preserving digital content are not unique to digital libraries. All resources in the digital format are fragile and susceptible to information loss. Multiple risks stem from the unstable nature of digital formats, degradation of storage media, and technological obsolescence. As the members of the Blue Ribbon Task Force on Sustainable Digital Preservation and Access note, digital preservation is a universal and "urgent societal problem".

In the context of digital libraries, the challenge of digital preservation is compounded by the structural complexity of digital objects and the interrelatedness of objects, collections, and repositories (Ross, 2012). The models and solutions for preserving content in present-day digital libraries will have an impact on future access to cultural heritage and scientific information. As Seadle (2008) emphasizes, "the digital libraries in 100 years will face problems that stem from the choices that we as librarians make today". Long-term preservation of digital content is recognized as a core function of digital libraries in the DELOS Manifesto (Candela et al., 2007), but it does not feature prominently in other definitions and frameworks. The practice of preserving digital objects has evolved since the first digital libraries were developed in the mid-1990s, but research in the area of digital preservation is relatively new (Chowdhury, 2010; Ross, 2012).

The concept and principles of preserving analog materials are well established in the library and archival community, although, as Cloonan (2007) points out, the institutional, custodial model is somewhat paradoxical in the modern world. Preservation is understood as an act of responsible custody aimed at preventing the deterioration of cultural heritage materials and restoring their usefulness and information value (Conway, 2007, 2010). Conway argues that the fundamental principles of digital preservation are the same as those of the analog world and define the priorities for ensuring the longevity and the useful life of information resources. The core concepts of preserving analog materials in regard to longevity, choice, quality, integrity, and access carry over to the digital environment, but the methods and practice are fundamentally transformed.

A comparison of analog and digital preservation approaches points to a continuum in principles but also highlights the distinct nature of preservation activities in the digital realm. In contrast to traditional practices, digital preservation is an urgent and ubiquitous issue. All digital objects, rather than selected items, are subject to preservation, although the level of activities performed on the object can differ. Digital objects are inherently more vulnerable than analog materials and require immediate attention from the point of creation. The standards and formats selected for encoding have implications for the quality and long-term maintenance of digital content. As Walters and Skinner (2010) stress, "the ways that objects are created, curated, and stored matter immensely in how preservation-ready they ultimately are".

Digital preservation needs to be ongoing with activities integrated into all phases of creating, managing, and storing information. Cloonan (2015) emphasizes the dynamic nature of the digital preservation cycle—that it is not linear and requires multiple actions. Lavoie and Dempsey (2004) point out that digital preservation is not an isolated activity but rather a set of practices diffused throughout the information lifecycle. In the analog world, conservation activities tend to occur toward the end of a resource's lifecycle. Once physical items receive conservation treatment and are stored properly, no additional attention may be required. In contrast, this type of "benign neglect" can be catastrophic for digital materials (Corrado and Moulaison, 2014; Ross, 2012; Walters and Skinner, 2010). Ross (2012) notes, "as a result of the constant evolution of technology, the degradation of storage media and the ever-increasing pace of 'semantic drift,' digital objects do not, in contrast to many of their analog counterparts, respond well to benign neglect". Digital preservation involves not only an active and continuous management of digital content but also monitoring of the evolving technological environment and preservation methods.

Digital preservation is a complex technical, social, economic, and organizational issue. Its complexity in digital libraries stems from the fact that it is interwoven into the process of creating, using, and maintaining a wide array of digital materials and collections. The sustainability of digital content depends on the careful management of preservation risks, organizational policies, institutional commitment, and technical infrastructure (Bradley, 2007; Corrado and Moulaison, 2014). Technical aspects have received a considerable amount of attention in the preservation community because of the immediate need of keeping intact files and protecting them from storage media failure and obsolescence. Increasingly, the researchers in the digital library field recognize that contextual information needs to be preserved along with the bitstream to render the bits as useful and meaningful objects (Beaudoin, 2012a; Chowdhury, 2010; Ross, 2012). Lesk (2014) captures the broader aspects of digital preservation by observing, "the greatest danger to digital materials is that we forget the meaning of them. Preservation depends on our knowledge: we may have bits but be unable to interpret them".

The field of digital preservation is still evolving, but significant progress has been made in building technological infrastructure and in developing policies, recommendations, and standards. The Task Force on Archiving Digital Information was established in 1994. The work of the Task Force resulted in a foundational report, which not only identified the critical challenges to preserving digital content but also provided a set of far-reaching recommendations (Waters and Garrett, 1996). The National Digital Information Infrastructure Preservation Program (NDIIPP) was formed by the Library of Congress in 2000. The National Digital Stewardship Alliance continues the work of NDIIPP, setting the agenda for national digital preservation and contributing to the development of standards and tools. Similar collaborative initiatives have been established in other countries with exemplary programs in the Netherlands and New Zealand (Library of Congress, n.d.). A number of research projects undertaken in Europe, including DELOS, Open Planets Foundation (currently Open Preservation Foundation), and Digital Preservation Europe, have had a significant impact on advancing the field of digital preservation (Ashenfelder, 2011; Brown, 2013; Library of Congress, n.d.). The last two decades of preservation research and practice resulted in developing more stable formats, preservation metadata standards, and trusted repositories.

CONCLUSION

This paper has established that digitization is an essential task in modern day libraries. If a library is to live up to current challenges, it has to go digital, that is, provide online services. This will enable it to preserve endangered library resources, improve the efficiency of information search mechanisms and enhance access to library resources. It is essential for the library management to provide policy guidelines and articulate plans for the exercise. Digital library, otherwise known as virtual library, has grown to a special field of study. Courses of instruction and research opportunities are now made available in this area of specialization by some university. As the GSDL and other allied softwares are available through open source and free of cost so if you have the training or acquire some knowledge from anybody regarding installation of this software and uploading of data then it can help you to work with digitization. For this purpose, scanner, digital camera, internet connection (for internet data upload and web hosting of this project), some dedicated skilled manpower.

QUESTIONS

1. Describe the process and Methods of digitial Libraries?
2. Explain the open source software for digitial libraries?
3. Define uses of Digital libraries ?
4. Define Digitization ?

5
Web Technology

INTRODUCTION

Web technology is the development of the mechanism that allows two of more computer devices to communicate over a network. For instance, in a typical office setting, a number of computers plus additional devices such as printers may be interconnected via a network, allowing for quick and convenient transmission of information. The processes involved in web technology are complex and diverse, which is why major businesses employ whole departments to deal with the issue. Web technology has revolutionized communication methods and has made operations far more efficient. Web Technologies involve the concept of a tier. A tier is nothing but a layer in an application. In the simplest form, the internet is a two tier application. They are the web browser and the web server. The technologies that exist in these tiers are as follows:

Client Tie: HTML, Java Script, CSS

Server Tier: Common Gateway Interface (CGI) Java Servlets, Java Server Pages (JSP), Apache Struts, Microsoft's ASP.NET, PHP, etc.

OBJECTIVES

- To provide a configurable and integrated interface to multiple resources
- To search across multiple databases

Advantage of web Technologies

- It offers convenience and a high speed of communication in the computer world. Whether in the office or the home, processes using a computer are more swift and straightforward with the use of a network.
- It allows messages to be sent around a system, whereas before it may have been necessary to employ a runner or leave your workspace to communicate a message.
- Web technology reduces costs and makes a company more efficient, raising business potential.

Disadvantage of web technologies

- Matters involving web technology can be very complicated, and it would be difficult for someone without relevant experience to sort a network problem out. This means it is necessary to employ someone with the specific skills to solve network issues, which costs money.
- Network security is another issue that must be considered when using web technology. Because weaknesses in a network could be exploited, important information could be stolen or destroyed and malware could infect the various network systems.
- The existence of a network provides the opportunity for an attack on the computers system

Web Browser

Meaning of Web Browser

A Web browser, also called a browser, is the program people use to access the World Wide Web. It interprets HTML code including text, images, hypertext links, Javascript and Java applets. After rendering the HTML code, the browser displays a nicely formatted page. The most popular Web browsers are Internet Explorer, Mozilla Firefox, Google Chrome, Opera and Apple Safari. All browsers are free and except for IE, which is Windows-only, they run on both Windows and Mac. Some browsers also run under Linux.

Basic Functions of Web Browser

The basic function of web browser is to retrieve a remote file from a web server and render it on the user's computer.

- To locate the file on the web server, the browser needs a Uniform Resource Locater. The URL can be typed in by the user, or it can be a link within an HTML page, or it can be stored as a bookmark.
- From the URL, the browser extracts the protocol. If it is HTTP, the browser then extracts from the URL the domain name of the computer on which the file is stored. The browser sends a single HTTP message, waits for the response, and closes the connection.
- If all goes well, the response consists of a file and a MME type. To render the file on the user's computer, the browser examines the MIME type and invokes the appropriate routines. These routines may be built into the browser or may be an external program invoked by the browser.

All browsers offer similar features, no matter which computer they run on. The way users interact with a Web page has more to do with the page than the browser. Web pages contain embedded programs that turn them into applications not much different than the software users install in their own computers.

Extending Browsers beyond the Web

Browsers were developed for the web, and every browser supports the webs basic protocols and few standard formats. However, browsers can be extended to provide other service while retaining the browser interface. Much of the success of browsers, of the web, and indeed of the whole Internet is due to this extensibility.

Mosaic and its successors have had the same three types of extensibility one for data types, one for protocols and one for the execution of programs.

(a) Data types

- With each data type, browsers associate routines to render files of that type. A few types have been built into all recent browsers including plain text, HTML pages and images in GIF format, but users can add additional types through mechanism such as helper application and plug-ins.
- A helper application is a separate program that is invoked by selected types of data. The source file is passed to the helper as data. For example, browsers do not have built-in support for files in the PostScript format, but many users have a PostScript viewer on their computer which is used as a helper application. When a browser receives a file of type PostScript, it starts this viewing program and passes to it the file to be displayed.
- A plug-in is similar to a helper application, except that is not a separate program. It is used to render source files of non-standard formats, within an HTML file, in a single display.

(b) Protocols

- HTTP is the central protocol of the web, but browsers

also support other protocols. Some, such as Gopher and WAIS, were important historically because they allowed browsers to access older information services. Others, such as Net News, electronic mail and FTP remain important.

- A weakness of most browsers is that the list of protocols supported is fixed and does not allow for expansion. Thus, there is no natural way to add Z39.50 or other protocols to browsers.

(c) Execution of programs

- An HTTP message sent from a browser can do more than retrieve a static file of information from a server. It can run a program on a server and return the results to the browser.
- The earliest method of archiving this was the common gateway interface (CGI), which provides a simply way for a browser to execute a program on a remote computer. The CGI programs are often called CGI scripts. CGI is the mechanism that most web search programs use to send queries from a browser to the search system. Publishers store their collections in databases and uses CGI scripts to provide user access.
- An informal interpretation of the URL http://www.dlib.org/chibin/seek?author=Arms is "On the computer with domain name www.dlib.org, execute the program in the file cgi-bin/seek, pass it the parameter string author Arms' and return the output". The program might search a database for records having the word arms in the author field.
- The earliest uses of CGI were to connect browsers to older databases and other information. By a strange twist, now that the web has become a mature system, the roles have been reversed. People who develop advanced digital libraries often use CGI as

a method to link the old system (the web) to their newer systems.

PARTS OF WEB BROWSER

Menu

- These menus will allow you to perform various tasks, such as print, save a favourite web page and set your internet options.

Function Icons

- Buttons that allow you to quickly perform tasks, such as print, refresh your web page, Search Engine Keyword Search 82 go back to the last page viewed or go forward to the next page viewed.

Minimize, Maximize, Close Buttons

- Allows you to make your browser smaller, larger or close your browser completely.

Web Address Area

- Type the web site address (or name0 in this box to go to that web site page and click go or hit the enter key on your keyboard. Eg.www.act.org/discover/login

Search Engine

- It is a large database containing information on millions of web sites, which allows you to enter keyboards to locate a site that offers the product or service that you seek.

Keyword Search Area

- Type the keywords to describe the type of information that you want to find.

Start Menu

- This menu will help you open various computer

software programs that you want to use, such as Microsoft Word or Internet Explorer.

Task Bar

- These lists all the programs that you currently have open. Click on one of the icons to maximize a particular program on your screen to continue working in that program.

INTERNAL ARCHITECTURE OF A WEB BROWSER

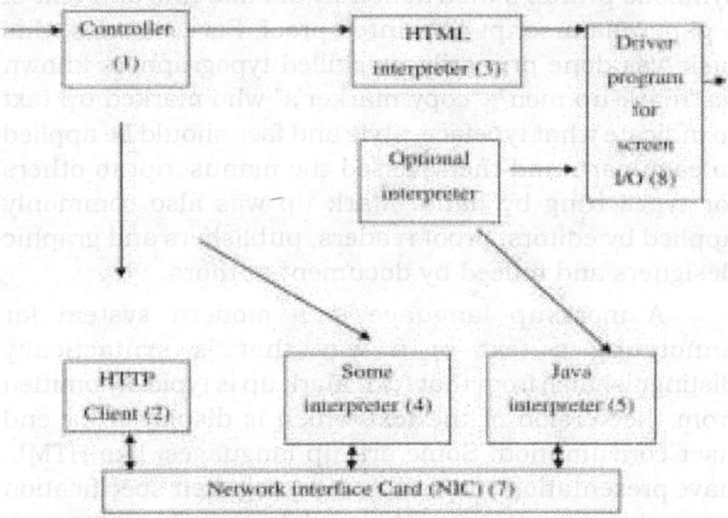

A browser contains pieces of software that are mandatory and some that are optional depending upon the usage. HTTP program shown in the above figure as (2) and HTML interpreter program (3) are mandatory. Some other interpreter programs as in (4), Java interpreter program (5) and other optional interpreter program (6) are optional. The browser also has controller, shown as (1) which manage all of them. The controller is like the control unit in a computer's CPU. It interprets both mouse clicks/selections and keyboard inputs. Based on these inputs, it calls the rest of the browser's components to perform the specific tasks. For e.g. when a user types a

URL, the controller calls the HTTP client program to fetch the requested Web page from a remote Web server whose address is given by the URL. When the web page is received, the controller calls the HTML interpreter to interpret the tags and display the Webpage on the screen.

MARK UP LANGUAGE

The term Mark Up is derived from the publishing practice "marking up" a manuscript, which involves adding handwritten annotations in the form of conventional symbolic printer's instruction in the margins and text of a paper manuscript or printed proof. For centuries, this task was done primarily by skilled typographers known as "mark-up men". "copy marker's" who marked up text to indicate what typeface, style and face should be applied to each part, and then passed the manuscript to others for typesetting by hand. Mark up was also commonly applied by editors, proof readers, publishers and graphic designers and indeed by document authors.

A mark-up language is a modern system for annotating a text in a way that is syntactically distinguishable from that text. Mark up is typically omitted from the version of the text which is displayed for end user consumption. Some ark up languages, like HTML, have presentation semantics, meaning their specification prescribes how the structured data is to be presented, but other mark-up language, like XML, have no predefined semantics.

A well-known example of a mark-up language is widespread use today is Hyper Text Mark-up Language (HTML), one of the document formats of the World Wide Web. HTML is mostly an instance of SGML and follows many of the mark up conventions used in the publishing industry in the communications of printed work between authors, editors and printers.

Types of Mark-up Language

There are general categories of electronic mark up: Presentational, procedural and descriptive.

Presentational Mark-up is that used by traditional word processing systems, binary codes embedded in document text that produced the WYSIWYG (What you see is what you get) effect. Such mark-up is usually designed to be hidden from human users even those who are authors or editors.

Procedural Mark-up is embedded in text and provides instruction for programs that are to process the text well known examples includes troff, Late X and PostScript. Popular procedural mark-up systems includes programming constructs, such that macros or subroutines can be defined and invoked by name.

Descriptive Mark-up is used to label parts of the document rather than to provide specific instruction as to how they should be processed. An example of descriptive mark-up would be HTMLs *tag, which is used to label a citation.*

Four Languages

XML

- XML stands for Extensible Markup Language much like HTML, structurally.
- XML is based on both SGML and HTML
- XML was designed to carry data, not to display data.
- XML tags are not predefined.
- XML is designed to be self-descriptive.

HTML

- HTML stands for Hypertext mark up Language and it is a plain text file which needs a simple text editor to create the tags.
- It is platform independent which means HTML

documents are portable from one computer system to another.

- HTML is the most widely used mark up language for web-based documents.
- HTML was designed to display data with focus on how data looks.
- Elements in HTML consist of alphanumeric tokens within angular brackets such as, <b>, <html>, <body>, etc. Most elements consist of paired tags/: a start tag and an end tag. For example, <b> is a start tag and </b> is an end tag.

SGML

- SGML stands for Standard Generalized markup Language.
- SGML is a Meta language which gives rise to other markup language.
- Programs based on SGML are very complex and expansive.

XHTML

- XHTML stands for Extensible Hypertext Markup Language.

SEARCH ENGINES

Search engine is an information retrieval system based web site that helps users to retrieve any information from huge internet database. It is a kind of tool that crawls in the web according to user direction and record everywhere and everything user look for. The search engine software is a kind of information retrieval program; it has two major tasks such as Searching through the billions of terms recorded in the index to find matches to a search and ranking retrieved records in order to decide most relevant.

COMPONENTS OF SEARCH ENGINE

Web Crawler (or Spider) : Programs that traverses the web from link to link, identifying and reading pages. It works as a network surfer and it downloads a searched web site to local disk.

- Web crawler is a kind of computer program that browses the Web in a methodical, automated way. This process is called as Web Crawling or spider. Search engines use spider to provide up-to-date information.
- The most important aim of web crawler is copying all visited web pages for later searches to make next searches faster.
- Web crawlers can also be used for automating maintenance task on a web site like checking links or validating code.
- Also web crawlers are used to collect specific information from Web pages, they finds million of documents and helps to IR systems to retrieve correct information in easy way.
- Also sometimes, crawler can find the information which is hidden by website owner or webmaster. Because of this, many web crawlers has to work according to robots exclusion protocol.
- Web crawlers also may work as link checker, page change monitor, validator, file transfer protocol client or web browser

TYPES OF SEARCH ENGINES

A search engine downloads all the information that the page contains and then examines that information to index keywords and phrases that can be used to categorise the sites. The exact method that it uses to do this and which information it looks at to create the index varies according to the search engine. Those words and phrases are added to the database alongside the URL and a description of the site. There are three types of search engine.

Active Search Engine

It collects web pages information by itself. It uses a program calls "Spider" or "Web Robot" to index and categorise Web pages as well as Web sites. The spider travels around the WWW in search of new sites and adds entries to their catalogue.

Passive Search Engine or Subject Directories

Search Engines of this type are possibly more accurately referred to as directories. It does not seek out web pages by itself. They rely on the WWW users to submit details on their site or their favourite sites in order to build up a database. For example. Yahoo Directory (www.yahoo.com) has 14 main subject categories and each of these categories has many sub categories and those sub- categories also contain their own sub-categories. Hierarchically organized directories tend to be smaller than those of the search engines, which mean that result lists tend to be smaller as well. Because subject categories are arranged by category and because they usually return links to the top level of a Website rather than to individual pages, they lend themselves best to searching for information about a subject rather than for a specific piece of information.

Due to the size of the web and constant transformation, keeping up with important sites in all subject areas is humanly impossible. Therefore, a guide by a subject specialist to important resources in his area of expertise is more likely than a general subject directory to produce relevant information and is usually more comprehensive than a general guide. These guides are known as Specialized Subject Directories. Such guides exist for virtually every topic. For examples:

- Voice of shuttle (http://vos.ucsb.edu) provides an excellent starting point for humanities research.
- Film buffs should consider starting their search with the Internet MOVIE database (http://us.imdb.com).

Meta Search Engine

An increasing number of search engine have led to the creation of "meta" search engine tools, often referred to as multi-threaded search engines. A Meta search engine does not catalogue any web pages by itself. It simultaneously searches multiple search engines. When a query is put before this type of search engines, it forwards that query to other search engines. There are two types of Meta search engines:

- One type searches a number of engines and does not collate the results. This means one must look through a separate list of results from each engine that was searched. It may present the same result more than once. Some engines require the searcher to visit each site to view the results. While others will fetch the results back to their own sites. When the results are brought back to the site, a certain limitation is placed on what is allowed to be retrieved. With this type of Meta search engine, one can retrieve comprehensive and sometimes overwhelming results. An example of this type of engine is Dogpile.
- The other type is more common and returns a single list of results, often with the duplicate hits removed. This type of Meta engine always brings the results back to its own site for viewing. In these cases, the engine retrieves a certain number of documents from the individual engines it has searched, cut off after a certain point as the search is processed. Other Meta search engines stop processing a query after a certain amount of time. Still others give the user a certain degree of control over the number of document returned in a search.

All these factors have two implications

- These Meta search engines returned only a portion of the documents available to be retrieved from the individual engines they have searched.
- Results retrieved by these engines can be highly relevant, since they are usually grabbing the first item from the relevancy-ranked list of hits returned by the individual search engines.

Some examples of Meta search engines are:

- Metacrawler (www.metacrawler.com)
- Surfwax (www.surfwax.com)
- Zapmeta (www.zapmeta.com)

Semantic Search Engines

Semantic Search engines are:

Semantic Web Search Engine (SWSE)

Semantic Web Search Engine is a search engine for the RDF Web on the Web, and provides the equivalent services a search engine currently provides for the HTML Web. The system explores and indexes the Semantic Web and provides an easy-to-use interface through which users can find the information they are looking for. Because of the inherent semantics of RDF and other Semantic Web languages, the search and information retrieval capabilities of SWSE are potentially much more powerful than those of current search engines.

Sindice

Sindice is a lookup index for Semantic Web documents built on data intensive cluster computing techniques. Sindice indexes the Semantic Web and can tell which sources mention a resource URI, IFP, or keyword, but it does not answer triple queries. Sindice currently indexes over 20 million RDF documents.

Watson

Watson allows you to search through ontologies and semantic documents using keywords. At the moment, you can enter a set of keywords (e.g. "cat dog old lady"), and obtain a list of URIs of semantic documents in which the keywords appear as identifiers or in literals of classes, properties, and individuals.

Yahoo Micro search

Micro search is Yahoo!'s stab at Semantic Web search and provides a richer search experience by combining traditional search results with metadata extracted from Web pages. Indexes RDF, RDF and Micro formats crawled from the Web. Micro search will soon be adding support for GRDDL.

Falcons

Falcons are a keyword-based search engine for the Semantic Web, equipped with browsing capability. Falcons provides keyword-based search for URIs identifying objects and concepts (classes and properties) on the Semantic Web. Falcons also provide a summarization for each entity (object, class, property) for rapid understanding. Falcons currently indexes 7 million RDF documents and allows you to search through 34,566,728 objects. Developed by IWS China.

Semantic Web Search

Powered by RDF Gateway, Intelli dimension's proprietary platform for Semantic Web applications and agents. Developed by Intelli dimension Inc.

Zitgist Search

The Zitgist Query Service simplifies the Semantic Data Web Query construction process with an end-user friendly interface. The user need not conceive of all relevant characteristics appropriate options are presented based on the current shape of the query. Search results are displayed through an interface that enables further discovery of additional related data, information, and knowledge. Users describe characteristics of their search target, instead of relying entirely on content keywords.

Swoogle

Searches through over 10,000 ontologies. 2.3 million RDF documents indexed, currently including those written in RDF/XML, N-Triples, N3(RDF) and some documents that embed RDF/XML fragments. Currently, it allows you to search through ontologies, instance data, and terms (i.e., URIs that have been defined as classes and properties). Not only that, it provides metadata for Semantic Web documents and supports browsing the Semantic Web. Swoogle also archives different versions of Semantic Web documents. Developed by the Ebiquity Group of UMBC.

Hakia

Hakia, which is a "meaning-based" search engine startup getting a bit of buzz. It is a venture-backed, multi-national team company headquartered in New York - and curiously has former US senator Bill Bradley as a board member. It launched its beta in early November this year, but already ranks around 33K on Alexa - which is impressive.

RSS SEARCH ENGINES

RSS takes a look at the specialized search tools that help you locate content in blogs, feeds and other sources of information. Many people mistakenly refer to RSS search as "blog search." While it's true that many blogs offer RSS feeds (automatic feed creation is a feature of most blogging software), not all blogs have feeds. Furthermore, RSS can literally be used with just about any kind of web-based content. RSS fundamentally is a relatively simple specification that uses XML to organize and format web-based content in a standard way.

Blogs Search Engines : Blog Search is search technology focused on blogs. It is a strong believer in the selfpublishing phenomenon represented by blogging. Blog Search helps users to explore the blogging universe more effectively and perhaps inspire many to join the revolution themselves.

Google Blog Search : Search function is an excellent way to find blogs. By using keywords just as would for a standard Google search and can sort the results by date.

Technorati : Technorati tracks over 100 million blogs and over 250 million pieces of tagged social media which means Technorati provides extremely comprehensive blog search results.

Sphere : Sphere is a great blog search engine that provides users the opportunity to sort results by time and relevance and also provides links to see related content to your search. One of the best features is one that allows users to view their search history.

Ice Rocket : Ice Rocket offers some very unique and helpful features. First, can enter your keywords then search within blogs, the web, MySpace, news or images. Second, can view the popularity of your keyword search using the Ice Rocket Blog Trends Tool.

Blog lines : Blog lines is a blog search engine and a feed reader. It provides features that allow users to search and subscribe to news feeds and blogs. Users can search for posts, feeds or citations.

Blog pulse : Blog pulse offers a wide variety of tools to help users find blogs and information including Buzz-tracker, trends search, blogger profiles, conversation tracker and more.

Blog Catalog : Blog Catalog is a social blog directory where anyone can search for information from blogs that have been submitted to the catalog.

E-BOOKS SEARCH ENGINES

- Ebooks Engines - http://www.ebook-engine.com/
- EBdb – Search Engine - http://www.ebdb.net/
- Elibrary - http://e-library.net/
- PDF eBook search engine – http://www.pdf-search-engine.com/
- Ebooksbayt - http://www.ebooksbay.org/
- Esnips Ebooks search engine - http://www.esnips.com/web/ebooksearchengine
- Fizziebooks - http://www.fizziebooks.com/

E-JOURNALS SEARCH ENGINES

- EEVL E-Jounal Search Engine (EESE) http://www.intute.ac.uk/sciences/ejournals.html
- Scirus - http://www.scirus.com/
- OJOSE -http://www.ojose.com/

EEVL E-JOUNAL SEARCH ENGINE (EESE)

Search the content of over 350 freely available full-text science, engineering and technology ejournals, selected for relevance and quality. Academic journals, trade publications, newsletters, and society journals are covered. All sites are also listed in the Intute: Science, Engineering and Technology catalogue of Internet resources.

SCIRUS E-JOURNALS SEARCH ENGINE

Scirus is the most comprehensive scientific research tool on the web. With over 450 million scientific items indexed at last count, it allows researchers to search for not only journal content but also scientists' homepages, courseware, pre-print server material, patents and institutional repository and website information.

OJOSE

Online Journal Search Engine is a free powerful scientific search engine enabling you to make search-queries in different databases by using only 1 search field. With OJOSE you can find, download or buy scientific publications (journals, articles, research reports, books, etc.) in up to 60 different databases.

ETD SEARCH ENGINE

Elsevier, world-leading publisher of scientific, technical and medical information products and services, is proud to announce the winners of the first awards for Electronic Theses and Dissertations (ETD) with the NDLTD-ETD Awards Powered by Scirus. Elsevier Journals Publishing and Scirus, the most comprehensive science-specific search engine, conducted the awards competition in partnership with the NDLTD (Networked Digital Library of Theses and Dissertations), the international organization dedicated to promoting the dissemination and preservation of electronic theses and dissertations, to sponsor this year's first-ever NDLTD-ETD Awards, which seek to recognize outstanding contributions to the body of electronically available ETD research.

The vast amount of information available on the Internet can make searching a long, Complicated process. The millennium search engines provide a more productive search by:

- Focusing only on sites with subject-specific data.
- Searching the "deep" web.
- Filtering out irrelevant data.

Library and Information Science professional should aware of invisible web tools and it helps to save the time and access to quality of information in short time.

SEARCH ENGINES CAN FURTHER BE CATEGORIZED BY SCOPE

General Search Engine : It covers a range of services and facilities Boolean search. E.g. Google, AltaVista

Regional search Engine : It refers to country specific search engines for locating varied resources region-wise. Examples Euro Ferret (Europe), Excite UK (UK), etc.

Subject Specific Search Engine : It does not attempt to index the entire Web. Instead it focuses on searching for Websites or pages within a defined subject area, geographical area or type of resources. Examples: Geo index (Geography/Environmental Science). Biochemistry Easy Search Tool (Biochemisry). Because this specific search engine aims for depth of coverage within a single area, rather than breadth of coverage across subjects, they are often able to index documents that are not included even in the largest search engines databases. Some examples of subject specific search engines are:

- www.123india.com Regional
- www.in.altavista.com Regional
- www.yahoo.co.uk Regional
- www.naukri.com Employment
- www.ndtv.com News
- www.zipcode.com Weather
- www.khoj.com India-specific

FEATURES OF SEARCH ENGINE: SEARCH ENGINES OFFER NUMEROUS FEATURES

When using a web search engine by entering more than one word, the space between the words has a logical meaning that directly affects the result of the search. This is known as the default syntax. For example, in Alta Vista, Infoseek and Excite, a search on the words : births migrations means that the searcher will get back documents that contain either the word "birds", then word migration or both. The space between the words defaults to the Boolean OR. This is probably not what the searcher wanted for this search.

Search engines return results in schematic order. Most search engines use various criteria to construct a term relevancy rating of each hit and present the search results in this order. ü Criteria can include: search terms in the title, URL, first heading, HTML tag; number of times search terms appear in the document; search terms appearing early in the document; search terms appearing close together. etc, Google page ranking algorithm displays mostly cited/hyperlinked Web sites/Web pages at the top of the screen.

One of the most interesting developments in search engine technology is the organisation of search results by concept, site, domain, popularity and making rather than by relevancy. Search engines that employ this alternative may be thought of as second-generation search services. For example:

- Direct Hit ranks according to sites other searches have chosen from their results to similar queries.
- Google ranks by the number of links from pages ranked high by the service.
- Inference Find ranks by concept and top-level domain.
- Northern Light sorts results into Custom Search Folders representing concepts and/or types of sites.

Often multiple pages are retrieved from a single site because all they contain the given search term. Alta Vista, Infoseek, HotBot, Northern Light and Lycos avoid this by a technique called results grouping, whereby all the terms from one site are clustered together into one result. It provides the opportunity to view all the retrieved pages from that chosen site. With these engines, one may get a smaller number of results from a search, but each result is coming from a different site.

Search engines do not index all the documents available on the web. For example, most search engines cannot index files to password-protected sites, behind firewalls or '96 configured by the host server to be left alone. Still other web pages may not be picked up if they are not linked to other pages and are therefore missed by a search engine spider as it crawls from one page to the next. Search engines rarely contain the most recent documents posted to the Internet, do not look for yesterday's news on a search engine.

Contents of database will generally not show up in a search engine result. A growing amount of valuable information on the web is not generated from the databases. This aspect of the Web is sometimes referred to as "the invisible Web" because database content is "invisible" to search engine spiders.

Some search engines allow users to viewed display of the retrieved Web sites/Web pages, clustered under different topics related to the search term(s). Examples include Kartoo (http: / /www.kartoo.com), Vivisimo (http:/ /www.vivisimo.com), etc.

FUNCTIONS OF SEARCH ENGINES

There are differences in the ways various search engines work but they all perform three basic tasks:

- They search the Internet by using specialized software called crawler or robot; these software/ agent can find out web pages by following hyperlinks.
- These agent/software send the cached version of web pages to the repository of a search (SE) and SE keeps an index of the words they find and where (URL) they find them.

SIGNIFICANCE OF SEARCH ENGINES

- User wants right information at the right time for the right cause in the right format at the right place.

- It is easiest way to group together and present numerous types of information and services that can be available to all kind of users.
- To improve the user-friendliness and to enable convenient access to the different kinds of information and services mounted on the web by users.

WEBSITE

Website designing requires many important tasks like discipline production in website and website maintenance. While designing a simple or modern web page, you must have many things in your mind. There are many important website design area like:

- Web graphic design
- Interface design
- Authoring
- User experience design
- Search engine optimization
- Standardized code and proprietary software

Tools and technologies

There are different tools and techniques used for designing webpage. It does not mean that all members in a team use the same tools and techniques for designing a webpage. While choosing your tool and technique for creating webpage, keep in mind all required things so that you will not face any problem in future.

Tools those are used for website designing:

- Pixate
- Affinity
- Avocode
- Antetype
- Sketch

- UXPin
- Form
- Macaw
- Marvel
- Webflow

Simple **technologies** used for website designing are:

- HTML / CSS
- Javascript
- php

Skills and technologies

Page layout

User interface design is totally affected by page layout. Page layout design of web page may be consistent or in consistent. For example, if you are designing a web page, you must set width and breadth same for each type of field. According to that page layout, units are sent to the web browser and which will be fitted into your browser display.

Marketing and communication design

Many type of markets are available that need to a website for successful run of their business. While designing website, you must keep in mind what type of website you are designing and what communication strategy they required. Web designers also keep in mind type of webpage like business to business website design, retail or entertainment website. Web designers must also consider the reputation of the business and owner in the market.

User experience design and interactive design

Web designer consider how the web page works and understand the working of web page. User experience is directly depends on the layout. If layout is well featured, user will come to your webpage again and again. As the interactive website is, user will use it more and more.

Typography

Web designers also use different type of font faces for their web pages. Web designers recognize specific number of safe fonts for all types of browsers.

Motion graphics

Page layout and user interface affected by motion graphics. Motion graphics create issues those are not initiated by the site browser.

Generated content

There are two ways to design a website. First one to design webpage is statistically or dynamically.

Static website stores all pages of a website and use them when they use that website while *dynamic website* runs on client side and saves all pages on server side to generate web pages.

Quality of code

Quality of code should be good so that there will not any failure during web page running. Poorly coded web pages sometimes causes crash while main running.

While designing any website or any type of apps, you must check what type of material you are using. In this article, we have provided 10 material design frameworks which are open source and you may use them freely.

1. Materialize CSS : Materialize is one of the first few web pages that has CSS in built feature and also offer some Google design guidelines. Materialize CSS is one of the complete package for developing small projects and html5 hybrid mobile apps. It includes color, typography, tables, grids and much important helper class. Materialize CSS is using with SASS so that you can download source scss files.

2. Material UI : Material UI is very professional and highly build framework that implements Google material design. This framework has been made in under the license of MIT, they maintains all new ensure changes and also acceptable for new additions in Material UI.

3. Bootstrap material design : This tool is basically used for new web page developers and who are bootstrap fans. Builder for bootstrap material design is Federico Zivolo. It comes packed with components and CSS packed compliant with guidelines for material design. Bootstrap material design is responsive website with fast speed. Elements in bootstrap including material design are

- Tabs
- Typography
- Buttons
- Navbars
- Progress bars
- Panels
- Sliders
- Bootstrap ready to use layout
- Responsive CSS3
- Grid system

4. Angular material : Angular material is a complete framework that implements Google material and have reusability and accessibility feature. All user interfaces are tested with this material design.

5. Polymer : Polymer is web based components build from W3C that allow collection of html, CSS and behavioral elements in best encapsulated package. Polymer is one of the future proof since it runs on the web components. You can also read for this material design on polymer-project.org.

6. MUI : This tool is under for MIT license, open source and free to use and is still under progress. You will get customize option for breakpoints, colors, font settings and etc. Framework MUI is under development but not production ready for purpose. **www.muicss.com** is website where you can read more about MUI material design.

7. Ionic material : Ionic framework is advanced framework for developing hybrid applications in HTML5. Features of this ionic material are:

- Option to develop reusable themes around it
- Option to extend ionic classes
- Ink effects as you interact
- Option to easily integrate with ionic directives.

ionicmaterial.com official website for this type of material design. You will get all detailed information about this on given website.

8. LumX : It is another framework for angular fans built with the help of SASS, neat query. It is responsive framework and uses core jQuery for better performance and no extra plugins required.

9. Nt1M / material framework : Nt1M is simple webpage framework that is used with any web page or with any app. You just need to add file to your project of you are using minimized version.

10. Paper : Paper is customizing theme that runs material design using bootstrap and web fonts from Google. You may also use different flavored themes in this framework.

WEB PORTALS

Portals are transformational tools that address the problem of information glut by customizing information content to meet specific end-user needs. The Web environment is growing in its importance as the preferred way of organizing and using information and for organizing work environments. Rapid advances in information technology point to the Web as the main framework for organizing information for work, research and e-commerce. The Web is rapidly becoming the preferred venue for information, financial transactions, document management and more. With the development of the World Wide Web, the "information search" has grown to be a significant business sector of a global, competitive and commercial market. Powerful players have entered this market, such as commercial internet search engines, information portals, multinational publishers and online content integrators. Will Google, Yahoo or Microsoft be the only portals to global knowledge in 2010? If libraries do not want to become marginalized in a key area of their traditional services, they need to acknowledge the challenges that come with the globalization of scholarly information, the existence and further growth of the academic internet.

Web portals are seen as positive potential frameworks for achieving order out of chaos. As portals become a primary means for transacting information and commerce, libraries of all types are becoming involved in thinking, planning and building various frameworks and services that they call portals. For many library customers, if what they need is not on the Web, it does not exist. Increasingly, information is available from alternative Web sources, and libraries have to compete with a diversity of new information services. If information is difficult to find using library tools and services, customers are looking for alternative sources – if they even think of libraries at all. This new reality translates into the need for making library Web environments effective and useful. This trend is especially challenging for libraries, who were and continue to see themselves as the traditional keepers of knowledge, which until very recently was housed in many millions of books and journals that are rapidly becoming digitized. We see a growing acceptance in libraries of Web portals as a framework for work and for Web services, as a way of increasing access to collections, learning and work.

The future of library websites lies in integration of different information management and services modules. Maintaining standalone modules with loosely integrated or moderately interoperable functions is too expensive for libraries. This is why libraries sought integrated systems in the first place. XML, web services, OpenURL, OAI-PMH, and the rapid development and approval of new standards are the true hope for the libraries. Perhaps we'll come to call them interoperable library systems, or even integrated library services.

Today managing library automation is now far more complex than the traditional maintenance of an integrated system. For instance, considering a standalone product, librarians should ask themselves and their vendors how this new product fits with existing efforts toward functional integration. Does the electronic resources management system know about the print journals? If considering a database portal, determine if it will use catalogued electronic resources. For digital access management systems, what can they accomplish that the cataloguing module cannot? If assessing a metasearch tool, find out if it can leverage the valuable features available from the various database providers. The digitization of publishing and the advent of the World Wide Web have resulted in the proliferation of a vast amount of content types and formats that include, but are not limited to, digitized collections, faculty and research groups' websites, conference web servers, preprint/e-print servers and, increasingly, institutional repositories and archives, as well as a wide range of learning objects and courses. If these resources are registered by a library at all, then they are in the form of separate lists of links or databases, but are not integrated into local digital library portals.

How should libraries see the future of their information discovery services? Instead of a highly fragmented landscape that forces users to visit multiple, distributed servers, libraries will provide a search index, which forms a virtual resource of unprecedented comprehensiveness to any type and format of academically relevant content. Libraries liaising with other partners are contributing ultimately to an open, federated search index network that will offer an alternative to the monolithic structures of current commercial information.com indexes.

PORTALS AND SUBJECT GATEWAYS

A general definition of a portal is "a Web site or service that offers a broad array of resources and services, such as e-mail, forums, search engines, and on-line shopping malls" (Webopedia). A variant is the vertical portal, or vortal, that typically provides news, research and statistics, discussions, newsletters, online tools, and many other services relating to a specific industry. This is nearer to the role in the development of the Resource Discovery Network (RDN is the UK's free national gateway to Internet resources for the learning, teaching and research community. The service currently links to more than 100,000 resources via a series of subject-based information gateways (or hubs). The RDN is primarily aimed at Internet users in UK further and higher education but is freely available to all) where a portal means a subject gateway that incorporates information from commercial sources, academic publishers and specialised databases, as well as current news and research. There is a consistency of approach that extends across different classes and formats, to include multimedia materials, directories, web pages, full-text databases, metadata and bibliographic records. Cross-searching across these resources is fundamental. There are various collections available of links to Internet resources - or more likely just to web sites - from the broad-based consumer-orientated services like Yahoo to those that deal with a particular subject, such as EEVL (EEVL is the Internet Guide to Engineering, Mathematics and Computing). They may be known as directories or gateways and the term 'subject gateway' is common in the UK education area for those that are centrally funded like SOSIG (Social Science Information Gateway) or BIOME (BIOME is a collection of gateways which provide access to evaluated, quality Internet resources in the health and life sciences, aimed at students, researchers, academics and practitioners) that arose from the JISC eLib Programme and deal with a particular area. More importantly, these UK examples evaluate and guarantee the academic quality of sites in order to exclude sources of questionable reliability.

NEED FOR THE PORTAL APPROACH TO LIBRARY WEBSITES

Libraries are rapidly expanding the Web-based delivery of content and related access services in order to meet the changing needs and expectations of their users. In the short 10-year period that the Web has existed, libraries have made great advances in their ability to provide Web-based access to a wide variety of information access services that were formerly only available within the walls of the library. Regardless of these advances, many library websites continue to replicate the physical and functional organization of the traditional library. Web-based access to services has evolved as a thin layer over library technical infrastructures that were designed to support traditional library services. As such, library websites are typically organized around library functions (interlibrary loan, circulation, reference) or existing information stores (the card catalogue, print indexes). Web-savvy users who are not familiar with traditional library organization methods do not view our websites as transparent or able to meet their information-seeking requirements. The common task of finding an article provides a useful example of the special knowledge of library organization and practices that is required to navigate a library website. The process begins with selecting a resource to search. Many users are overwhelmed when faced with deciding which information resource will best suit their current needs and may select a resource for less than optimal reasons. Once an information resource is selected, the user must often master another complex interface to search for appropriate material. Upon identification of an item of interest the user must determine if it is owned or licensed by the library, possibly remember that interlibrary loan is available and in the worst case report an item as missing from the shelf.

Developing an understanding of changing user demands and the basic building blocks of a new architecture will be a challenge in our current technical environment where systems are organized around data (e.g., the catalogue, vendor-based indexes and publishers) or services (e.g., interlibrary loan, circulation and reference). One approach is to design multi-tiered architectures that include an integration layer providing programming-level services for user-level applications such as a portal.

The National Science Foundation has identified and recommended a cyber-infrastructure that will be necessary to suit the needs of scientists in the future. The cyber infrastructure specifies a service layer that includes several components relevant for libraries that support scientific research and education. They are calling for the specification of services that will provide access to data, information and knowledge management services. In addition, they are requesting the specification of collaboration services that will support the emerging collaborative processes necessary within the sciences .

While undoubtedly successful in offering integrated access points, from the library point of view one gets the impression that there is still some development to be done in order to build real end-user services that find the full acceptance of researchers and students. In the era of popular Internet full text search indexes these projects are focussing mainly on metadata by giving reference information about the resource (e.g. a certain server or database) rather than searching within the content sources (such as the full text itself). The records of all these portal databases, which usually describe intellectually selected content sources, can of course be used as a valuable starting point. To support the changing user demands within the Web-based service paradigm, technical infrastructures must be made available to users in a manner that supports their tasks. The library portal is one approach to organizing information resources and services in a way that supports the users' needs. However, the library portal will not be the only starting point for access to the library. Other systems, such as course management systems and enterprise portals, may also serve as primary access points for users engaged in a variety of different information gathering tasks. The library portal, along with other application-level interfaces that provide consolidated access to multiple underlying systems, must have integrated connections to every system and information resource.

The importance of subject gateways - and portals as they develop - to the hybrid library will be readily apparent from the underlying commitment to collation of quality assured web resources. In their relatively short existence the gateways have done much to raise the profile of the importance of quality assurance with respect to web resources in higher education, as well as fulfilling their fundamental role of easily accessible navigational aids to such resources, arranged by subject.

Successful library systems will need to be designed as a set of core functional components that can be repurposed to suit the requirements of all user-level service needs and made available to a variety of application-level interfaces. Hence a library portal is defined as a web-based tool that provides a customizable interface to information aggregated from a variety of sources of a particular library with parent organization's mission and goals. Portals are implemented as application-level interfaces and based on software suites that provide integrated access to information resources and related services. Library websites integrate predominantly online library catalogues and databases with some full text repositories (e.g. e-journals). Freely available academic online content as described above is usually not covered by library portals. If they are selected at all they are mainly organized as html-link lists or specific databases that record reference metadata about web repositories.

Beyond online catalogues, databases and e-journals, researchers started to place their pre-prints or post-prints on the websites of faculties and research groups. Comprehensive web servers of scientific congresses include online presentations and papers, large international pre-print servers, often organized by the scientific community, store thousands and hundreds of thousands of documents, and the creation of e-learning objects is gaining increasing popularity.

WEBPAGE DESIGN USING HTML

This wikiHow teaches you how to write a simple web page with HTML (hypertext markup language). HTML is one of the core components of the World Wide Web, making up the structure of web pages. Once you've created your web page, you can save it as an HTML document and view it in your web browser. Creating an HTML page is possible using basic text editors found on both Windows and Mac computers.

Adding a Head to Your HTML

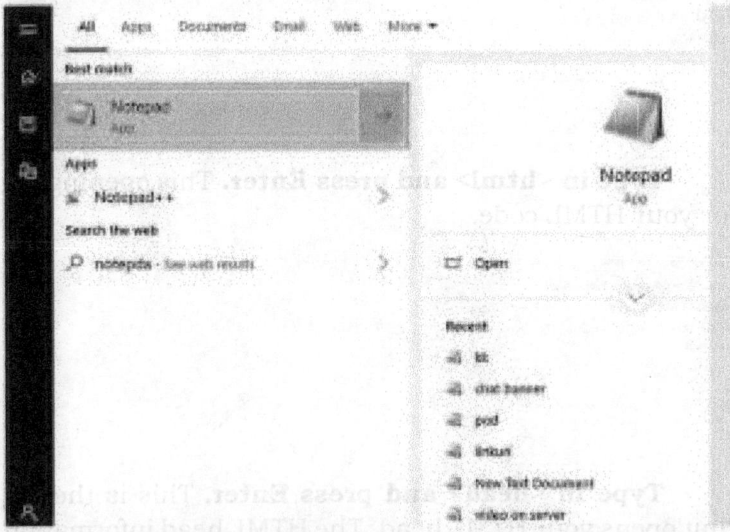

Open a text editor : On a computer running the Windows operating system, you'll usually use Notepad, or Notepad++ whereas macOS users will use TextEdit:

Windows - Open **Start**

, type in notepad, or notepad++ and click **Notepad** or "Notepad++ or sublime" at the top of the window.

macOS - Click **Spotlight**

, type in textedit, and double-click **TextEdit** at the top of the results.

Type in <!DOCTYPE html> and press µ! Enter. This tells the web browser that this is an HTML document.

Type in <html> and press Enter. This opening tag for your HTML code.

Type in <head> and press Enter. This is the tag that opens your HTML head. The HTML head information that is not usually displayed on your web page. This information can include, the title, meta data, CSS style sheets, and other scripting languages.

Type in <title>. This is the tag to add a title to your page.

Type a title for your web page. This can be any title you want to name your web page.

Type in </title>and press Enter. This is the tag to close your title tag.

Type </head> and press µ! Enter. This is the tag to close your head. Your HTML code should look something like this.

ADDING A BODY AND TEXT TO YOUR HTML

Type in <body> below the closed "Head" tag. This tag opens the body of your HTML document. Everything that goes in the HTML body displays on the web page.

Type in <h1>. This is the tag to add a heading to your HTML document. A Heading is large bold text that typically goes at the top of your HTML document.

Type a heading for your page. This can be the title of your page or a greeting.

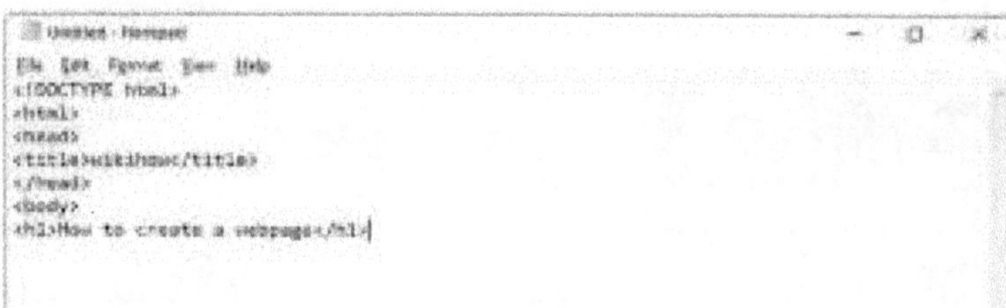

Type </h1> after your heading text and press µ! Enter. This tag closes your heading.

Add additional headings as you go. There are six different headings that you can create by using the <h1></h1> through <h6></h6> tags. These create headings of different sizes. For example, to create three different-sized headings in succession, you might write the following:

```
<h1>Welcome to My Page!</h1>
<h2>My name is Bob.</h2>
<h3>I hope you like it here.</h3>
```

The headings shows the priority or importance of the text. But its not necessary to use a higher heading if you want to use any lower heading. One can directly use H3, even if there is no H1 in your post.

```
<!DOCTYPE html>
<html>
<head>
<title>wikiHow</title>
</head>
<body>
<h1>How to create a webpage</h1>
<p>
```

Type <p>. This is the tag to open a paragraph. Paragraph text is used to display normal sized text.

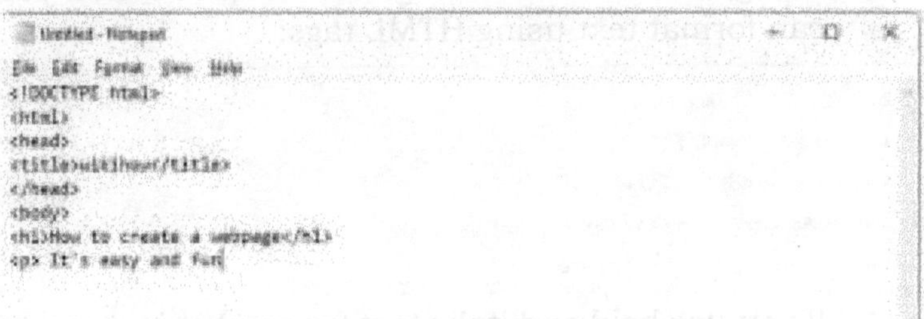

```
<!DOCTYPE html>
<html>
<head>
<title>wikiHow</title>
</head>
<body>
<h1>How to create a webpage</h1>
<p> It's easy and fun
```

Type some text. This can be a description for your web page or any other information you wish to share.

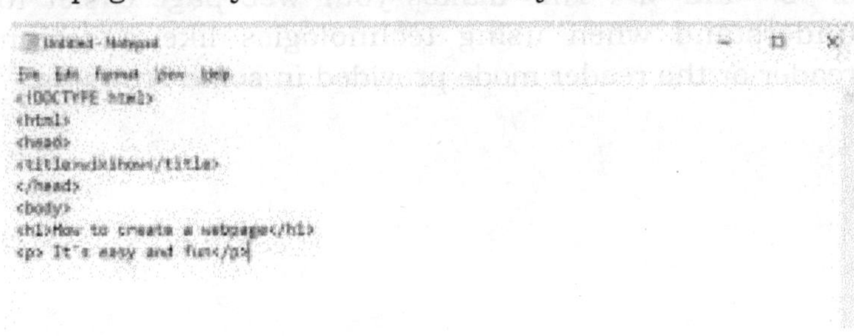

```
<!DOCTYPE html>
<html>
<head>
<title>wikiHow</title>
</head>
<body>
<h1>How to create a webpage</h1>
<p> It's easy and fun</p>
```

Type </p> after your text and press µ! Enter. This the tag to close your paragraph text. The following is an example of paragraph text in HTML:

```
<p>This is my paragraph.</p>
```

- You can add multiple paragraph lines in a row in order to create a series of paragraphs under one heading.
- You can change the color of any text by framing the text with the <font color="color"> and </font> tags. Make sure to type your preferred color into the "color" section (you'll keep the quotes). You can turn any text (e.g., headers) into a different color with this set of tags. For example, to turn a paragraph's text blue, you would write the following code: <p><font color="blue">Whales are majestic creatures.</font></p>
- You can add bolds, italics and other text formats using HTML. The following are examples of how you can format text using HTML tags:

```
<b>Bold text</b>
<i>Italic text</i>
<u>Underlined text</u>
<sub>Subscript text</sub>
<sup>Superscript text</sup>
```

If you use bold and italic text for emphasis, not just for styling, use the <strong> and <em> elements instead of <b> and <i>. This makes your web page easier to understand when using technologies like a screen reader or the reader mode provided in some browsers.

ADDING ADDITIONAL ELEMENTS TO YOUR HTML

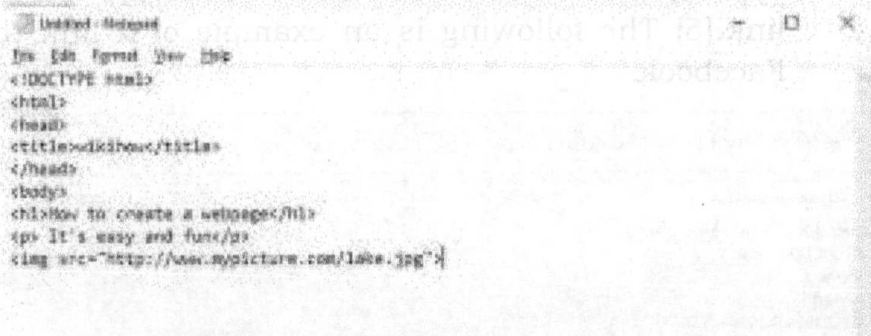

```
Untitled - Notepad
File Edit Format View Help
<!DOCTYPE html>
<html>
<head>
<title>wikihow</title>
</head>
<body>
<h1>How to create a webpage</h1>
<p> It's easy and fun</p>
<img src="http://www.mypicture.com/lake.jpg">
```

Add a picture to your page. You can add an image to your HTML using the following steps:

- Type <img src= to open your image tag.
- Copy and paste the image URL after the "=" sign in quotation marks.
- Type > after the image url to close your image tag. For example, if the image's URL is "http://www.mypicture.com/lake", you would write the following:

```
<img src="http://www.mypicture.com/lake.jpg">
```

```
Untitled - Notepad
File Edit Format View Help
<!DOCTYPE html>
<html>
<head>
<title>wikihow</title>
</head>
<body>
<h1>How to create a webpage</h1>
<p> It's easy and fun</p>
<img src="http://www.mypicture.com/lake.jpg">
<a href="https://www.facebook.com">Facebook</a>
```

Link to another page : You can add a link to your HTML using the following steps:

- Type <a href= to open your link tag.
- Copy and paste URL after the "=" sign in quotation marks.
- Type > after the URL to close the link portion of the HTML.

- Type a name for the link after the closing bracket.
- Type </a> after the link name to close the HTML link.[5] The following is an example of a link to Facebook.

```
<a href="https://www.facebook.com">Facebook</a>.
```

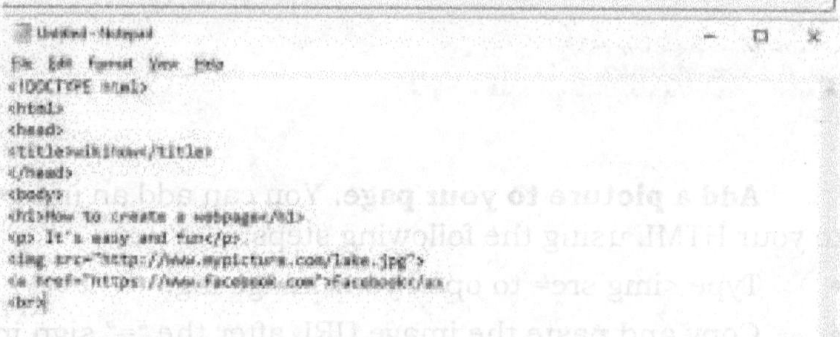

Add a line break to your HTML. You can add a line break by typing <br> to your HTML. This creates a horizontal line that can be used to divide different sections of your page.

CLOSING YOUR HTML DOCUMENT

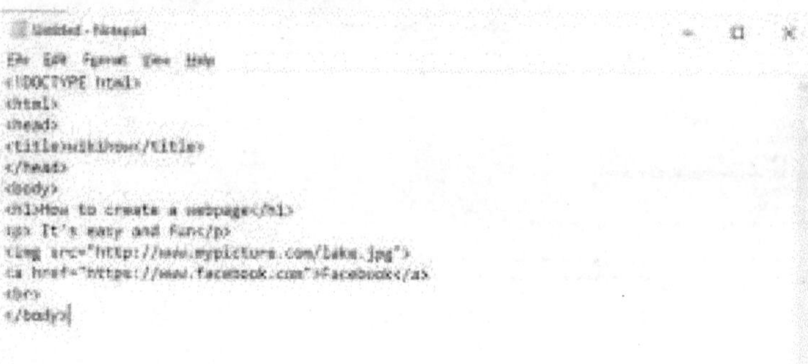

Type </body> to close your body. After you have finished adding all your text, images and other elements to the body of your HTML document, add this tag at the bottom of your HTML document to close the body of your HTML document.

```
Untitled - Notepad
File Edit Format View Help
<!DOCTYPE html>
<html>
<head>
<title>wikihow</title>
</head>
<body>
<h1>How to create a webpage</h1>
<p> It's easy and fun</p>
<img src="http://www.mypicture.com/lake.jpg">
<a href="https://www.facebook.com">Facebook</a>
<br>
</body>
</html>
```

Type </html> to close your HTML document. This tag goes below the tag to close your HTML body at the end of your HTML document. This tells the web browser there is no more HTML code after this tag. Your entire HTML document should look something like this:

```
<!DOCTYPE html>
<html>

<head>
<title>wikiHow Fan Page</title>
</head>

<body>

<h1>Welcome to My Page!</h1>
<p>This is a fan page for wikiHow. Make yourself at home!</p>

<h2>Important Dates</h2>
<p><i>January 15, 2019</i> - wikiHow's Birthday</p>

<h2>Links</h2>
<p>Here is a link to wikiHow: <a href="http://www.wikihow.com">wikiHow</a

</body>
</html>
```

CONCLUSION

The library portals need to provide new search and navigation interfaces or improved ranking and display features for academic content. Vendors of integrated library systems have partly responded to this development and offer already separate local and central modules. New requirements for libraries have resulted in the set-up of new systems such as digital library systems, digital collection and e-print servers. The increase of systems alongside with the increased demand on financial and staff resources to maintain these systems have led to discussions within libraries and on a campus wide level in order to find out how these systems interact with each other and investigate potential duplication or even multiplication of services implemented in different systems. The current Grid-research initiatives, that address distributed, large-scale computing in a wider context, could provide valuable technology for the building of distributed data and access networks. Libraries will need to watch closely these developments and be open for collaborations.

QUESTIONS

1. Define Tools and Technique of web sites ?
2. Describe Web Technology ?
3. Define how to add Text to HTML page ?
4. List the type of search engine ?

References

- Arms, W.Y. (1995). Key concepts in the architecture of the digital library. D-lib Magazine, July, 1995. URL: http://www.dlib.org/dlib/July95/07arms.html
- Chapman, S. and Kenny, A.R. (1996). Digital conversion of research library materials: a case for full informational capture. D-lib Magazine, October, 1996. URL: http://www.dlib.org/dlib/october96/cornell/10chapman.html
- Chepesuik, R. (1997). The future is here: America's libraries go digital. American Libraries, 2(1), 47-49.
- Erway, R.L. (1996). Digital initiatives of the Research Libraries Group. D-Lib Magazine, December, 1996. URL: http://www.dlib.org/dlib/december96/rlg/12erway.html
- Graham, P.S. (1995a). Requirements for the digital research library. URL: http://aultnis.rutgers.edu/texts/DRC.html www.purl.org.
- Reitz, J. M. (2008). OOHS – Online dictionary for library and information science. Retrieved 15 July 2008 from http:Mu.com/odlis/
- Ibrahim Usman Alhaji. (n.d.). DIGITIZATION OF LIBRARY RESOURCES AND THE FORMATION OF DIGITAL LIBRARIES: A PRACTICAL APPROACH.
- Gonçalves, M.A.; Fox, E.A.; Watson, L.T.; Kipp, N.A. 'Streams, Structures, Spaces, Scenarios, Societies (5S): A Formal Model for Digital Libraries'. ACM Transactions on Information Systems (TOIS), 22(2), 270 –312, 2004
- Alexa T. McCray and Marie E. Gallagher. Principles For Digital Library Development. Communication of the ACM COMMUNICATIONS OF THE ACM, 2001, 44(5): 49-54.

- Chore, N.V. and Salwe, S.M. Library Sources and Service In Digital Environment. Proceeding of state level seminar on role of information technology in library, Karad (8-9 April 2010).
- R.K. and Vishwanthan K.R. Digital Libraries: development and principles, Library Review, 2001, 50 (1): 10-16.
- Cleveland G. (1998). Digital Libraries: Definitions, Issues and Challenges, IFLANET, UDT Occasional Paper # 8, March, 1998. URL: http://www.ifla.org/VI/5/op/udtop8/udtop8.htm
- Dillon A. (2002). Technologies of Information: HCI and the Digital Library, Human Computer Interaction in the New Millennium edited by John M. Carroll, Published by Pearson Education Asia, pp 457-474.
- Dumais, S.T., Platt, J., Heckerman, D. and Sahami, M. (1998) "Inductive learning algorithms and representations for text categorization." Proc ACM Conf on Information and Knowledge Management, pp. 148–155.
- Erway R.L. (1996). Digital initiatives of the Research Libraries Group. D-Lib Magazine, December, 1996. URL: http://www.dlib.org/dlib/december96/rlg/12erway.html (Accessed on 12 Dec. 2003).
- Ali Shiri.(2003) Digital library research: current developments and trends. Library Review, 2003,52(5): 198-202.
- Ranganathan, S.R.. Five Laws of Library Science. 1999. Sarada Ranganathan Endowment Publications.
- R.K. and Vishwanthan K.R. (2001) Digital Libraries: development and principles, Library Review, 2001, 50 (1): 10-16.
- Seaman, David, (n.d.). Aggregation, integration and openness: current trends in digital libraries. In International Symposium on Digital Libraries and Knowledge Communities in Networked Information Society (DLKC'04).
- Sujin, B. (2003). Basic issues in digital libraries: The 21st century knowledge centers. Hyderabad: Professional Books Publishers.
- Weeks, A. C. (2003). The International Children's Digital Library. Presented at the 69th IFLA world Library and Information Congress 1-9, Berlin.
- Bush, V., "As We May Think", Atlantic Monthly, July 1945, pp. 101-108.

- Association of Research Libraries. Proceeding of 126th ARL annual meeting, 1995. http:// ar1.enLorg/arl/proceedings/ 126/2-defn.htmi.
- Kent (Allen). Encyclopedia of Library and Information Science. Vol. 62; 1998; p215-17.
- Craft (B) eta1. Providing government information on the Internet: Experiment with THOMAS: In proceeding for geographically of digital libraries conference. DL 95, Austin TX. June 12-15, 1995, p19-25.
- Arora, (Jagdish). Building digital libraries: An overview. DESIDOC Bulletin of Information Technology. Vo1.21 (6); 2001; p3-24.
- Marchiomini (G). Information Seeking in electronic environments. New York, Cambridge Press, 1995.
- Richvalsky; Walkins. Designing and implementing a digital Library. ACM Crossroad student magazine. Jan 1998. http:/ / www.acm.org/crossroads.rds5.2/ digital.html.
- Kent (Allen). Encyclopedia of Library and Information Science. Vol. 63; 1998, p259-77.
- Wiederhold (G). Mediation in the architecture of future information systems. IEEE Computer. Vol. 38-49; March 1992.
- Arora, Jagadish (2001) Building digital Libraries : An overview DESIDOC bulletin of Information technology 21; 3-24
- Army w y (1995) key concepts in the architecture of the Digital Library. D Library Magazine July @ttp:llwww.dlib. oreanization.iulv95/07armsShtml)
- Schatz, Bmee R (1997) Information retrieval in digital libraries, bringing search to the net. Science .275 ; 327-33
- Suleman, H. and Fox, E.A. (2003), "Leveraging OAI harvesting to disseminate theses", Library Hi Tech, Vol. 21 No. 2, pp. 219-27.
- Needlman, M. (2000), "Z39.50 – a review, analysis and some thoughts on the future", Library Hi Tech, Vol. 18 No. 2, pp. 158-65.
- Nelson, M.L., Rocker, J. and Harrison, T.L. (2003), "OAI and NASA's scientific and technical information", Library Hi Tech, Vol. 21 No. 2, pp. 140-50.
- Paepcke, A., Chang, C., Garcia-Molina, H. and Winograd, T. (1998), "Interoperability for digital libraries worldwide",

Communications of the ACM, Vol. 41 No. 4, pp. 33-43.

- Shen, R. (2006), "Applying the 5S framework to integrating digital libraries", dissertation for the Doctor of Philosophy in Computer Science and application, Virginia Polytechnic Institute and State University, Blacksburg, VA.
- Kaczmarek, J. and Naun, C.C. (2005), "A statewide meta-search service using OAI-PMH and Z39.50", Library Hi Tech, Vol. 23 No. 4, pp. 576-86.
- Lagoze, C. and Van de Sompel, H. (2001), "The open archives initiative: building a low cost interoperability framework", Proceedings of the Joint Conference on Digital Libraries, Roanoke VA, June, available at: www.openarchives.org/documents/oai.pdf (accessed 5 August 2007).
- Ding, H. and Solvberg, I. (2007), "Rule-based metadata interoperation in heterogeneous digital libraries", The Electronic Library, Vol. 25 No. 2, pp. 193-206.
- Fox, E.A. and Marchionini, G. (1998), "Toward a worldwide digital library", Communications of the ACM, Vol. 41 No. 4, pp. 29-32.
- Green, N., Ipeirotis, P.G. and Gravano, L. (2001), "SDLIP þ STARTS¼SDARTS A protocol and toolkit for meta-searching", Proceedings of the JCDL'01, June 24-28, Roanoke, VA, pp. 207-214.
- Bearman, D. (2007), "Digital libraries", Annual Review of Information Science and Technology, Vol. 41, pp. 223-72.
- Field, R. (1979), "The library as publisher", Library Association Record, Vol. 81 No. 8, pp. 383-5.
- Fox, E. and Urs, S.R. (2002), "Digital libraries", Annual Review of Information Science and Technology, Vol. 36, pp. 503-89.
- Heery, R. (2000), "Information gateways: collaboration on content", Online Information Review, Vol. 24 No. 1, pp. 40-5.
- Kaushik Anna, Podcasting in library environment. Annals of Library and Information Science, Vol.57, June 2010, pp122-129.
- Mahesh, G. and Mittal, R. (2008), "Digital libraries in India: a review", Libri, Vol. 56 No. 1, pp. 15-24.
- McMenemy, D. (2007), "Less conversation, more action: putting digital content creation at the heart of modern

librarianship", Library Review, Vol. 56 No. 7, pp. 537-41.

- Terri Muraski, (2016). Improving e-resources management, together, Journal of Electronic Resources Librarianship, 285-286.
- Marilyn White & Susan Sanders, (2009). E-Resources Management: How We Positioned Our Organization to Implement an Electronic Resources Management System, Journal of Electronic Resources Librarianship, 183-191.
- Vinod Kumar, Vandana, D.K. Batra, (2018). Usage pattern of e-resources among management students in Nagpur, Maharashtra (India), The Electronic Library.
- David McMenemy, (2012). Emergent digital services in public libraries: a domain study, New Library World, Vol. 113 Iss 11/12 pp. 507 – 527.
- Ilka Datig, (2018). Revitalizing library websites and social media with content strategy: Tools and recommendations, Journal of Electronic Resources Librarianship, 63- 69.
- Martin Zimerman, (2011). E-books and piracy: implications/ issues for academic libraries, New Library World, Vol. 112 No. 1/2, 67-75.
- Michael Breaks, (1999). Management of electronic information, Proceedings of the IATUL Conferences.
- William Johnston, Jin Guojun, Case Larsen, Jason Lee, Gary Hoo, Mary Thompson, Brian Tierney, Joseph Terdiman, (1997). Real-Time digital libraries based on widely distributed, high-performance management of large data objects, International Journal of Digital Library, 241–256.
- Bansode, S., & Pujar, S. M,Scholarly Digital Library Initiatives: World Versus India. DESIDOC Journal of Library & Information Technology, 28(6),(2008),21-26.
- Varatharajan, N., &Chandrashekara, M, Digital Library Initiatives at Higher Education and Research Institutions in India. Library Philosophy and Practice, (2007), 1-7.
- Mittal, R., & Mahesh, G. Digital libraries and repositories in India: an evaluative study. Program, 42(3), (2008), 286-302.
- Oehlerts, B., &Liu, Digital preservation strategies at Colorado State University Libraries. Library Management, 34(1/ 2),(2012),83-95.
- Jones, M, The digital preservation coalition. VINE, 34(2), (2004), 84-86.

- Biswas, G.& Paul, D. An evaluative study on the open source digital library softwares for institutional repository: Special reference to Dspace and greenstone digital library, International Journal of Library and Information Science, 2(1), (2010), 1-10.
- Arms, W. Y. Digital Libraries. Boston, MA: MIT Press, 2000. Bowman, C. M. et al. The Harvest Information Discovery and Access System. Computer Networks and ISDN Systems 1995:28(1&2), 119–25.
- Buck, A. M., Flagan, R. C. and Coles, B. Scholars' forum: a new model for scholarly communication. Mar. 1999 (http://library.caltech.edu/publications/scholarsforum/).
- Building a 'GenBank' of published literature. Science 2001:23 Mar., 2318–19.
- Judson, H. F. Structural transformations of the sciences and the end of peer review. Journal of the American Medical Association 1994:272(2), 92–4.
- Lagoze, C. and Van de Sompel, H. The Open Archives Initiative: building a low-barrier interoperability framework. Proceedings of the First ACM/IEEE Joint Conference on Digital Libraries, Roanoke, VA: JCDL, 2001, pp. 54–62, also at www.openarchives.org/documents/ oai.pdf.
- Powell, A. An OAI approach to sharing subject gateway content. WWW10 Poster Track (www.rdn.ac.uk/publications/www10/oaiposter/).
- PubMed Central. An NIH-operated site for electronic distribution of life sciences research reports. Aug. 1999 (www.nih.gov/welcome/director/pubmedcentral/pubmedcentral.html).
- Van de Sompel, H. and Lagoze, C. The Santa Fe Convention of the Open Archives Initiative. D-Lib Magazine 2000:6(2) (www.dlib.org/dlib/february00/ vandesompel-oai/02vandesompel-oai.html).
- Davis, Eric T. An overview of the access and preservation capabilities in digital technology. http:Ilwww.iwaynet.net/-lscildiglibldigpapf f.html
- Rusbridge, Chris. Towards the hybrid library. D-Lib Magazine, JulylAugust; 1998. http:llwww.dlib.org/dlib/july98/rusbridge. html
- Fox, E. & Marchionini, Gary. Towards a worldwide digital library. Communication of the ACM, 1998, 41(4), 29-32.

- Guthrie, Kevin M. JSTOR: From project to independent organisation. D-Lib Magazine, JulylAugust, 1997. http:/ lwww.dlib.org/dlib/july97/07guthrie. html
- School of Scanning, 3-5 Nov., 1997, New York. Papers and presentations. Northeast Document Conservation Center, Andaver, MA, 1997.
- Hulser, Richard P. Digital library: Content preservation in a digital world. DESIDOC Bulletin of Information Technology, 1997, 17(6), 7-14.
- Borgman, Christine L. (1999). What are digital libraries? Competing visions. Information Processing and Management. 35, p. 227- 243
- Eileen Mathias. (2004). Anatomy of a digitization project. Library Journal, 129(1), S2.
- FAO. (2010) Digital libraries, repositories and documents .Information Management Resource Kit (IMARK).
- Hopkinson, Alan. (2009). Library automation in developing countries: The last 25 years. Information Development. 25, p. 304. DOI: 10.1177/0266666909349678
- Keller, M.A. (February 2009). Establishing a digital library. [White Paper]. Sun Microsystems, Inc.
- Singh, G., Mittal, R., & Ahmad, M. (2007). A bibliometric study of literature on digital libraries. The Electronic Library., 25(3), pp. 342-348
- Digital Library Federation. (2001), Registry of Digitized Books and Serial Publication,
- Ding, Choo Ming. (2000), Access to Digital Information: Some Breakthrough and Obstacles, Journal of Librarianship and Information Science, Vol.32 No.1
- Smith, Abbey (2001), Strategies for Building Digitized Collection. Washington, D.C. Digital Library Federation, Council on Library and Information Resources.
- O'Mahony, S. (2003). Guarding the commons: how community managed software projects protect their work. Research Policy, 32(7), 1179-1198.
- Open Source Initiative (OSI). 2012. Retrieved from http:// opensource.org/
- New Zealand Digital Library. 2012. Retrieved from http:// www.nzdl.org/custom/howto2/collect/book/pdf/How_to_build_Preface.pdf

- Digital Libraries. 2012. Retrieved from ftp://ftp.cordis.europa.eu/pub/ist/docs/rn/castelli.pdf
- Madalli, D. P. (2003). A digital library of library and information science using DSpace.
- DSpace 1.8 System Documentation. (2012) .Retrieved from: http://www.dspace.org/.
- Tansley, R., Bass, M., Stuve, D., Branschofsky, M., Chudnov, D., McClellan, G., & Smith, M. (2003, May). The DSpace institutional digital repository system: current functionality. In Proceedings of the 3rd ACM/IEEE-CS joint conference on Digital libraries (pp. 87-97). IEEE Computer Society.
- INFORMATION TECHNOLOGY –DIGITAL COMPRESSION AND CODING OF CONTINUOUSTONE STILL IMAGES – REQUIREMENTS AND GUIDELINES. 1992. Retrieved from http://www.w3.org/Graphics/JPEG/
- Edmund, B. (2012). DSpace 1.8 Documentation.Retreived from: https://docs.prosentient.com.au/prosentientjspui/handle/1 / 74?mode=full&submit_simple=Show+full+item+record
- Bass, M.J. et al. (n.d). DSpace –A Sustainable Solution for Institutional Digital Asset Services-Spanning the Information Asset Value Chain: Ingest:Manage, Preserve, Disseminate: Internal Reference Specification Functionality, version 2002-03-01. Retrieved from http://libraries.mit.edu/dspacemit/technology/functionality.pdf
- Open Archives Initiative. (2012). Retrieved from http://www.openarchives.org/
- EPrints WIKI. (n.d). Retrieved from http://wiki.eprints.org/
- "Open Archives Forum. (n.d.). Comparison of DSpace and Eprints". Retrieved from http://www.oaforum.org/resources/tvtoolscomp.php
- Jayakanth, F. (2002). Eprints.org Open Archive Software (EAS): An Overview [PowerPoint slides]. Retrieved from: http://www.ncsi.iisc.ernet.in/raja/opendl/easoverview.pdf
- Barve, S. A. (2012). An evaluation of open source software for building digital libraries. Retrieved From:
- DSpace System Documentation. 2011. Retrieved from https://wiki.duraspace.org/display/DSDOC18/DSpace+System+Documentation
- Witten, I. H., Bainbridge, D., & Boddie, S. J. (2001, January).

Power to the people: end-user building of digital library collections. In Proceedings of the 1st ACM/IEEE-CS joint conference on Digital libraries (pp. 94-103). ACM.

- Greenstone Overview. 2012. Retrieved from http://www.greenstone.org/manuals/gsdl2/en/html/Chapter_overview_of_greenstone.html
- Isah, Abdulmumin; Serema, Batlang Comma; Mutshewa, Athulang; Kenosi, Lekoko (2013). "Digital Libraries: Analysis of Delos Reference Model and 5S Theory". Journal of Information Science Theory and Practice. 1 (4): 38–47. doi:10.1633/JISTaP.2013.1.4.3.
- Fox, Edward A. (1999). "The Digital Libraries Initiative: Update and Discussion". Bulletin of the American Society for Information Science. 26 (1). ISSN 2373-9223. Archived from the original on 3 April 2018. Retrieved 30 April 2018.
- Choudhury, G.G. (2004). Access to Information in Digital Libraries: Users and Digital Divide, International Conference on Digital Libraries Knowledge Creation, Preservation, Access and Management, New Delhi,(1),56-64.
- Das, T. K., Sharma, A.K., & Gurey, P. (2009). Digitization, Strategies & Issues of Digital Preservation: An Insight View to Visva-Bharati Library. 7 th International CALIBER © INFLIBNET centre, Pondicherry University, Puducherry, Ahmadabad.
- Das. U. (2006). Importance of preserving historical materials of Assam. New Spectrum, 2(1), 15- 24.
- Ganzha, M., et.al (2010). Combining information from multiple search enginespreliminary comparison. Information Science 180(10): 1908-1923, retrieved on December 14, 2012 from http://dx.doi.org/10.1016/j.ins.2010.01.010
- Gupta, S., & G. Singh. (2006). Management of digital libraries: Issues and strategies. Journal of Library and Information Science 13(1). 1
- ICPSR. Digital Preservation Strategies. Retrieved on December 10, 2012 from http:// www. i cps r. umi ch .edu/ dpm/ dpm- en g/ terminology/strategies.html
- Jain, P.K., & Praveen Babbar. (2006). Digital libraries Initiatives in India. The International Information & Library Review, 38, 161-169.
- Jones, C., Zenios, M., & Markland, M. (2003). Digital Resources in Higher Education: Pedagogy and Approaches

to the use of digital resources in Teaching and Learning, Northern Ireland. Retrieved from http://www.ifets.info/journals/10_1/6.pdf.

- Kaur, P., & S. Singh. (2005). Transformation of traditional libraries into digital libraries: A study in the Indian context. Herald of Library Science 44(1–2), 33–39.
- Kemp, B., & Jones, C. (2007). Academic Use of Digital Resources: Disciplinary Differences and the Issue of Progression revisited. Educational Technology & Society, 10 (1), 52-60.
- Malaghan, C.A., & Chowdappa. (2012). Tools and Techniques to explore search Engines and Databases, National Conference on Trends in Developing & Managing E-resources in Libraries, 184-185.
- Mahesh, G., & Mittal Rekha. (2008). Digital Libraries in India: A Review, National Institute of Science Communication and Information Resources, New Delhi, 58, 15– 24.
- Meitei, L.S., & Devi, P. (2009). Open Source Initiative in Digital Preservation: The Need for an Open Source Digital Repository and Preservation System. 7th International CALIBER © INFLIBNET centre, Pondicherry University, Puducherry,
- Parekh, Y.R., & Parekh, P. (2009). Planning for Digital Preservation of Special Collections in Gujarat University Library. 7th International CALIBER © INFLIBNET centre, Pondicherry University, Puducherry, 20. Praveen Singh, C. (2008). Digital Libraries Tool & Techniques, Alfa Publication, New Delhi.
- Sanjay Kumar, S. (2006). Microfilm: a digital archiving method of preservation. New Spectrum. 2 (1), 7-14.
- Arnold, Stephen (2004), 'Information boundaries and libraries' viewed 4 Nov. 2005,
- Lakos, Amos A. (2004), 'Portals in Libraries', Bulletin of the American Society for Information Science and Technology, vol. 31, no. 1.
- Lossau, Norbert (2004), 'Search Engine Technology and Digital Libraries: Libraries Need to Discover the Academic Internet', D-Lib Magazine, vol. 10, no.6

WEBSITES

- (http://www.loc.gov/standards/mets)
- http://www.dli.ernet.in/
- http://www.vigyanprasar.gov.in/digilib/
- http://www.ncert.nic.in/textbooks/testing/Index.htm
- http://www.ignca.nic.in/dlrich.html
- http://ignca.nic.in/ndb_0001.htm
- http://www.namami.org/index.htm
- http://www.muktabodhalib.org/digital_library.htm
- http://shodhganga.inflibnet.ac.in/)
- http://www.vidyanidhi.org.in/
- www.ias.ac.in/pubs/journals/
- www.insa.ac.in
- http://nopr.niscair.res.in/
- IndMED@NIC: http://indmed.nic.in
- http://www.inflibnet.ac.in/ojs/
- www.medknow.com/journals.asp
- www.krepublishers.com/KRE-New-J/index.html
- www.openarchives.org
- http://oaisrv. nsdl. cornell.edu/Register/RegisterSite.pl
- https://www.sun.com/offers/details/digital_libraries.xml
- http://www.imarkgroup.org
- http://www.digilib.org/collections
- http://117.240.228.70/handle/10603/3731
- (http://www.technorati.com)
- (http//www.icerocket.com/?tab=blog)
- (http://www.bloglines.com)
- (http://www.blogpulse.com)